"Carolyn is a terrific writer...ruggedly ....g.
If you're looking for a self-help book, look elsewhere. If you're looking for a friend to take a journey with...this book makes pleasant company."

> Don Miller, author
> *Blue Like Jazz*

"The kind of person who can write spendid, honest, moving, thoughtful, inspiring songs isn't always the kind of person who can write books of the same nature. But Carolyn Arends can do both. This book is a masterpiece album of chapters that will make your heart sing. It will do your heart good by stimulating your mind, your imagination, and your faith."

> Brian McLaren, author/activist

"Carolyn observes keenly, reflects deeply, and renders it all poetically. She can startle with her honesty. We're used to all that in her music, in her capacity as songwriter. These pages are a reminder that God is often nearest when he seems furthest, most bent on our remaking when we think he's bent on our undoing—and that sometimes these are one and the same thing."

> Mark Buchanan, pastor, author
> *The Rest of God*

"Exquisite writing combine with humble self-disclosure and profound insight to make this book an unforgettable experience."

> Brennan Manning
> *The Ragamuffin Gospel* and *Abba's Child*

"Anyone who has tired of hearing famous Christians discuss their faith with trite platitudes will appreciate Arends' refreshing book...Arends addresses the eternal nature of the soul and affirms the powerful grace of God."

> *Publisher's Weekly*

"This is a terrific read…gut-wrenchingly honest and vulnerable. She shares her highest highs and her lowest lows, including her doubts—doubts we all share about God, His mysterious ways, even those times He seems absent. The lure of Arends' book is that it doesn't neatly resolve life's tough issues with pat answers, but despite—and even because of—these unresolved mysteries, her faith grows that much stronger. As a result, so did mine—as will anyone's who reads this book."

Mike Moring, editor
Christianity Today

"Wow. I knew Carolyn had the ability to move me, I just didn't know how far. This work is excellent. It is comforting. It is honest. In *Wrestling with Angels*, Carolyn gently reminds us that Jesus reigns supreme in all our contradictions and riddles. It is a message we need desperately. A beautiful work."

Margaret Becker
recording artist

"Surely there's another book like it, but even I, an ardent reader, can't name any work so free, precise, and real as *Wrestling with Angels*. The outlook of Carolyn Arends is contagious: don't quench doubts or fears or routine, for therein lies mystery (meaning God revealing Himself)…The adventure called life gets a fun, belief-drenched spin from Carolyn Arends, a gifted writer who truly is living the questions."

Josh M. Shepherd, cmusicweb.com

"Like her literary heroes, from Chesterton to L'Engle, Carolyn Arends illuminates the precarious intersection of the human and the holy. This most artful collection of stories and essays proves that she can run with the giants. *Wrestling with Angels* is warm and funny and absolutely relentless in pursuit of why it all matters."

Billy Crockett, recording artist

"Carolyn's book came as an unanticipated gift. I didn't know she could write a book, really. But she can—beautifully—and I finished the book feeling much encouraged to move again into the mystery of relationship with a shattering God."

Ashley Cleveland, recording artist

"As Carolyn gives voice to our unspoken questions, we feel as if we finally have a chance to lay it all out on the table, an opportunity for a hearing of our deepest concerns, and a safe vent to air our troublesome thoughts. But she doesn't leave us pondering, scratching our heads, and puzzling over divine mysteries. By assuming the Almighty is big enough for our questions, Carolyn enlarges our view of the God who may not always choose to answer in a manner we consider timely, but who still sends us dazzling red rocks in our dullest wilderness days. Provocative, stirring, emotional, and true, *Wrestling with Angels* leads us to the place where hard truths and holy secrets intersect."

Lorilee Craker, journalist/author

"Frederick Buechner calls a religious book 'a transparency.' In *Wrestling with Angels* Carolyn Arends is transparent and poetic through her prose, insightful and gutsy in her honest sharing, and often laugh-out-loud-funny and poignant. I will be buying copies for all my friends."

Lisa Tawn Bergren, author

"*Wrestling with Angels* is a seamless continuation of Carolyn's magnificent writing—deceptively simple avenues to the thoughtful and profound. Carolyn is a great writer. I loved this book."

Steve Bell, singer/songwriter

"Soul-baring honesty is the strength Carolyn brings to her work. That, and great humor and tremendous writerly gifts."

Ron Reed, *Canadian Christianity*

"What a wonderful book! I could not put it down! Carolyn's writing is both humorous and heart-piercing...I was moved to laughter and tears several times just in the first few pages! For me, this book was a reminder of how BIG God is, but how incredibly involved He is in even the SMALL details of our lives."

Christie Barnes

"If good storytelling is always a liberating force for the reader, then Carolyn's intimate and kind observations and anecdotes are pure emancipation. Arends has left pretense disheveled in the corner where it belongs and opens her Christian journey to us in a way that is at once disarmingly candid and decidedly edifying. There is a grace about this book in the patience (and even pleasure) it takes in celebrating what makes us grandly and haltingly human, and in that celebration, it makes space for and offers hope to believers who too often confuse frailty and finitude with sin or failure. I'm proud to add my 'amen' to this work."

Dwight Ozard

"Loosed from the constraints of three-and-a-half minute songs, Carolyn gently expounds and expands on a precious truth: Our unanswered questions—in and of themselves, in all of their maddening, puzzling, frustrating glory—provide evidence of the most profound Answer we can ever hope to receive. Through her engaging storytelling she relates her journey into the Mystery via those unanswered questions, subtly encouraging us to take the trip, too."

Rose Capanna, writer
His Place

Wrestling
with
Angels

Carolyn Arends

HARVEST HOUSE PUBLISHERS

EUGENE, OREGON

Carolyn Arends: This work published in association with the Conversant Media Group, PO Box 3006, Redmond, WA 98007.

ConversantLife.com is a trademark of Conversant Media Group. Harvest House Publishers, Inc., is a licensee of the trademark ConversantLife.com.

Cover by Abris, Veneta, Oregon

WRESTLING WITH ANGELS
Formerly *Living the Questions*
Copyright © 2000 by Carolyn Arends
Published 2008 by Harvest House Publishers
Eugene, Oregon 97402
www.harvesthousepublishers.com

Library of Congress Cataloging-in-Publication Data

Arends, Carolyn.
   [Living the questions]
   Wrestling with angels / Carolyn Arends.
      p. cm.
   Originally published: Living the questions. Eugene, OR. : Harvest House Publishers, ©2000.
   ISBN-13: 978-0-7369-2061-2
   ISBN-10: 0-7369-2061-7
   1. Arends, Carolyn. 2. Christian biography—Canada. 3. Contemporary Christian musicians—Canada. I. Title.
   BR1725.A764A3 2008
   277.1'082092—dc22
   [B]

                                                            2007028428

Printed in the United States of America

08 09 10 11 12 13 14 15 16 / VP-PH / 10 9 8 7 6 5 4 3 2 1

For my brother Chris...
who has always had the courage to let the
Mystery be a mystery.

For Mark...
I am inexpressibly glad to be living the
questions with you

¤

And for Ben...
thank you for walks by the lake.
Stay on the path, Little Man.

And now for Beth...
you are my sunshine,
and a wrestling angel,
if ever there was one.

Your mommy loves you both.

Download a Deeper Experience

Carol Arends is part of a faith-based online community called ConversantLife.com. At this website, people engage their faith in entertainment, creative arts, science and technology, global concerns, and other culturally relevant topics. While you're reading this book, or after you have finished reading, go to www.ConversantLife.com/carolynarends and use these icons to read and download additional material related to the book.

 Resources: Download study guide materials for personal devotions or a small-group Bible study.

 Videos: Click on this icon for interviews with Carolyn and video clips on various topics.

 Blogs: Read through Carolyn's blog and articles and comment on them.

 Podcasts: Stream ConversantLife.com podcasts and audio clips from Carolyn.

conversant life .com

engage your faith

Contents

Problem and Paradox

Living the Questions

Postlude

Wrestling

"So what's your book about?"

I t's a fair question, one that's provoked a remarkably wide variety of answers throughout the seven years since this book was first released. It's often asked the way a restaurant patron asks about the chicken. *Is it spicy? Will it give me heartburn? How big are the portions?* I'm never sure how to answer. "It depends on your palate and your hunger," I want to say, but I know that's evading the original question. What *is* this book about?

"It's about having a faith that not only survives but

thrives in the midst of unanswered questions," I sometimes reply. If the inquirer looks confused, I attempt a little more specificity. "It's also about the time my dad sold our Impala to some missionaries. And the day we adopted my little brother." If the person seems at all interested, I go a little further. "It's about the prairie drought of 1972, my mother-in-law's Alzheimer's, an overbearing telephone pole near my old junior high school, and the sweltering summer I thought I lost my faith."

"Oh," the questioner says, backing away slowly.

Still, sometimes people read the book in spite of my descriptions. Sometimes they see that it is a collection of stories about the Mystery I find myself caught in. Sometimes they even find something of their own stories in the pages. I love it when that happens, and I wish I could call up all the people who have read this book and ask them if *they* know what it's about. But I suspect that might be an unprecedented and slightly inappropriate approach. Also, I don't have most of their phone numbers. So I keep trying to figure it out on my own.

Every once in a while I develop a new theory. A few years ago a flurry of books was released that documented the way a postmodern shift in thinking was forcing Christians to consider the idea that some mysteries should be embraced rather than solved. "Aha!" I thought. "My book is about what happens when a girl raised in answer-oriented modernism crashes into a question-obsessed, postmodern world." Of course, I know if you use the word "postmodern," you aren't. Still, I stand with one foot in modernism and the other in postmodernism, and I think it's fair to say this book is at least partly an account of what happens when a notoriously inflexible girl is forced to do the splits.

There are other theories too. If reading new cutting-edge books has given me a fresh understanding of my story, reading musty old books has done the same. Over the years I have found myself drawn increasingly to contemplative writers, from the early desert fathers to more recent guides such as Merton and Nouwen, and I've finally had the epiphany I should have had long ago. "Aha! My story is about what happens when a girl raised in fundamentalism slowly realizes she has the spiritual temperament of a Christian mystic." In that sense, this book is about learning to live in my own skin, learning to know and love the God of both Revelation and Mystery with the particular inclinations He's given me, and learn ing not to worry so much if my journey is more dark night than daybreak.

The "dark night" business leads me to a third theory, my current favorite. I've begun to see this book as the chronicles of times spent on the banks of the Jabbok River. I am speaking metaphorically, of course. Near my house is the Fraser River, and it would take serious financial incentive (and an industrial-strength mosquito net) to get me to spend even one night on its mucky shores. But if you know the book of Genesis, you'll recognize the Jabbok River. It's the place where Jacob—dreamer, schemer, patriarch, scoundrel, and, according to

Scripture, one of our earliest spiritual ancestors—wrestled with God and lived to tell the tale.

It is of very great comfort to me that Jacob and so many of the men and women listed in Hebrews 11 *"Faith Hall of Fame"* are, when you really read their stories, a total mess. Right away, in the first book of His Book, the Author of the Universe establishes a consistent pattern of choosing the most unlikely, least-qualified candidates to make covenants with, to write salvation history with. As a group, these Giants of Faith are more prodigal than pilgrim, more sinner than saint. They fuss, they falter, they flounder, they fail. Their résumés often include adultery, deceit, murder, and worse. (Of course, their biographies also sometimes include shining moments of belief, commitment, obedience, and sacrifice, but never mind that for now. I'm trying to make a point here.)

My kids love to watch the animated show *The Berenstain Bears*, which is about a family of rather articulate and hygienic bears and the world they inhabit. "They're kind of furry around the torso," goes a line of the bluegrassy theme song. "They're just like people, only more so."[1] Sometimes, reading about the patriarchs and matriarchs, I find myself humming that tune. They're just like us, only more so. They dream big, they fall far, they learn the hard way that God is larger than they are and they can't out-sin His grace (try as they might). In the final analysis, they don't give up on God; much more importantly, He doesn't give up on them. But in the meantime, they dance in a two-steps-forward, three-steps-back kind of rhythm I find awfully familiar.

Jacob is like the others, only more so. He comes from good stock; Abraham (aka "The Father of Nations") is his grandfather, and Isaac and Rebekah are his parents. He's a bit of a mama's boy, smart and bookish, not into hunting. His brother, Esau, is a man's man, straightforward and robust, great at catching game. Genesis 25:28 gets the family dysfunction out into the open with a directness Dr. Phil would find both refreshing and appalling: "Isaac, who had a taste for wild game, loved Esau, but Rebekah loved Jacob."

They're twins, Jacob and Esau. My mom once knew a family who named their twin boys "Pete" and "Repeat." (Child welfare officials took the parents to court and made them legally change the names, but at home they were still "Pete" and "Repeat.") Isaac and Rebekah give their boys only marginally better handles. "Esau" means "Hairy"; by all accounts Isaac's firstborn son has the complexion of a goat. "Jacob" means "Deceiver"; the second-born son arrives grasping the heel of his seconds-older brother in a rivalry apparently begun in the womb. Isaac loves "Hairy," Rebekah loves "Deceiver," and the family favoritism and contention are key ingredients in a recipe for disaster.

There is an obsession with blessing in Jacob's story. Not blessing as in "Gesundheit!" or "Thank You, Lord, for the food." Not even blessing as in the Southern "Bless her heart" (which means, translated loosely, "Oh dear, look at her outfit"). In Jacob's story, blessing is something tangible and essential, something worth obtaining at any price. When it is given (parent to child or Creator to creature), the blesser not only gives love and acceptance, he passes on a significant aspect of his own life and legacy. The blesser knows that the blessing is, in the words of Frederick Buechner, "The conveying of something of the very energy and vitality of his soul to the one he blesses."[2] Jacob wants the blessing. He'll grab it like he grabbed his brother's heel. He won't let go.

But a blessing is like the love it contains. It can't be bought or forced or stolen. And though Jacob infamously impersonates Esau and successfully tricks his blind old father into giving him the firstborn's blessing, the wind still whistles through the spaces that should have been filled by genuine fatherly affection and acceptance. Psychologists claim that people who never receive the family blessing often become workaholics, ceaselessly striving for the approval they were denied at home. Jacob becomes *Exhibit A*, as successful and driven as he is alienated from everyone around him.

Esau wants to kill him, naturally, for stealing the blessing, so Jacob flees to Paddan Aram, where his Uncle Laban lives. Laban has a daughter named Rachel, and Jacob falls for her instantly. Jacob and Laban strike a deal—Jacob will provide seven years of labor and his reward will be Rachel. But when the wedding night arrives at last, Laban (who is even more of a deceiver than his nephew) switches his unloved older daughter, Leah, for Rachel. Twenty years later Jacob finds himself with four unhappy wives (two contentious sisters and their hand-maidens) and a whole brood of brawling kids. It's a sad story, and more than a little sordid. But God, apparently, does not avert His eyes. Jacob is still His man. God is still Jacob's God. Even if Jacob doesn't always know it.

Jacob's work ethic and intelligence allow him to become a successful herdsman, and he makes both his uncle and himself extremely wealthy. Eventually he wearies of Laban's constant attempts to cheat him and decides it's time to go home and face the family. It's been 20 years since he's seen the mother who loves him and the father who doesn't. More to the point, it's been 20 years since he and Esau have been within striking distance of each other. Has the passage of time cooled or intensified his brother's rage? No doubt Jacob's head tells him to go anywhere but home. But his heart can't take the estrangement anymore, and he decides it's worth the risk. He packs up the wives and kids, rounds up the servants and the flocks, and sneaks off without telling Laban goodbye.

Jacob makes his way southwest, back to Canaan, back to the land God promised to him even while he was on the lam. He is resolved to get the resolution he has been so long denied. He is clear-eyed, determined, ready for whatever may come...until he gets close to home—close enough to know it's only a matter of days or even hours before he is face to angry face with the (much bigger) brother he cheated.

Reading the story, you can feel the pressure building.

Is that pounding Jacob hears the march of an enemy army or the sound of his own heart hammering in his chest? Is that eerie movement on the horizon a hostile brother or a tree in the wind? Jacob sends some of his men ahead with a conciliatory message for Esau. The messengers return with news Jacob doesn't want to hear. Esau is on his way to meet him, and he's brought along 400 of his closest, toughest friends.

The story reaches a fever pitch. Jacob, we are told, is in "great fear and distress." He divides his party into two camps, thinking that way he can spare at least half the group. He sends goats, sheep, camels, cattle, and donkeys ahead for his brother, hoping that the gifts might placate him. And he prays one of the first real prayers of his life, a classic "distress prayer" familiar to anyone who's ever found himself in a serious bind, begging God to spare his life and the lives of his family.

He sets up camp on the swampy banks of the Jabbok River and tries to rest, knowing he'll need his strength in the morning. But sleep won't come. I imagine he keeps tweaking the plan, rehearsing the past, dreading the future, trying to pray, working to calm his breathing and pull it together. Sometime in the night he decides his family might be safer if they're not with him. After all, he's the one Esau wants. In the inky darkness he shakes his wives and children awake and urges them to the other side of the river. Now he's alone.

Suddenly, wordlessly, there is another form in the darkness. *Is it Esau? It must be Esau.* The man grabs him, pins him to the ground, and Jacob knows this is it. His attacker has the strength of a hundred men and the fury of a thousand. Jacob struggles beneath his weight, sure he'll be dead in a minute. What goes through his mind? Does he think of his mother weeping for her son? Of his children finding their father lifeless in the chill of the dawn? Of Rachel? *Oh, Rachel...*

Jacob finds his own might and fights back. He is astonished to discover that this night he too has the strength of a hundred men and the desperation of a thousand. For a moment he even has the advantage. He wraps his trembling hands around Esau's neck and realizes with a shock this can't be Esau. It's been 20 years, but he knows the smell and feel and size of his brother. Who is this man?

Whoever he is, he's strong and fast. But Jacob is too. So evenly are they matched that the struggle lasts minutes, then hours, until both men are drenched in sweat and blood and Jabbok mud. Even as the sun begins to rise, they thrash about, silent save for the sound of ragged breathing and the occasional thud of impact or grunt of effort. Inside Jacob a gut-wrenching dread is growing, deeper than even the fear of his brother. Is he afraid he'll lose? Or...afraid he'll win?

The stranger settles the matter for him, touching his leg in a deft, oddly gentle move that dislocates Jacob's hip. A searing pain rips through his body, but worse, he realizes he can no longer put his weight on his leg. Now he is holding on to his attacker not to overpower him but to keep from falling. At last the man speaks.

"Let me go, for it is daybreak," he says.

But Jacob does not let go. He shakes his head. He is surprised to hear his own voice in a hoarse whisper: "I will not let you go unless you bless me."

Somehow, somewhere in that long, silent struggle, Jacob has come to know he is wrestling not with his brother, not with any man, but with *Something Other*. An angel? Maybe. The notes in my Bible refer to Jacob's adversary as an "Angel of the Lord." But if you read the story all the way through, it's clear Jacob is convinced that he is grappling, in some life-shattering and life-resurrecting way, with *Yahweh Elohim*, with God Himself. Is it hearing the voice that makes Jacob know? Or catching a glimpse of the Stranger's face in the first light of dawn? Maybe it is the intimacy of that violent embrace, hour after exhausting hour, that makes Jacob finally realize Who he is dealing with. However he knows...he *knows*. And now he hangs on out of need and longing. He hangs on because he cannot stand alone and because he cannot let go.

Jacob has God in his arms, and God has Jacob in His. Of all the things Jacob could ask for—strength to face his brother, healing from his pain, safety for his family—he asks for a blessing. This is the part that makes me cry. He asks for a *blessing*. The love and acceptance of God, a chance to have something of His life. Jacob is willing to die for it. He's willing to live for it too.

"What is your name?" the man asks.

"Jacob," he answers.

Then the man says, "Your name will no longer be Jacob, but Israel, because you have struggled with God and with men and have overcome."

And then the Bible tells us, "He blessed him there."³

At long last Jacob gets his true blessing. He doesn't get it by grasping, by scheming, by deceiving, or even by achieving. He gets it by defeat. And he gets a new name too, as part of the blessing. He is no longer Jacob, the Deceiver. Now he is Israel, the God-wrestler. Imagine that. God names not just Jacob, but His people, His nation, His church: Israel. God wrestlers.

My book may indeed be about postmodernism and about mysticism, but I've come to see that mostly it is about wrestling. It is about the realization that when a creature encounters the Creator of the Universe, the divine embrace is likely to feel more like a deathgrip than anything else. As much as I long for more direct encounters with *Yahweh Elohim*, I should be careful what I wish for. Jacob was fortunate to walk away with only a limp. If God seems sometimes maddeningly hidden, it may very well be for my own safety.

Still, here is an intriguing piece of the Good News: I am a spiritual descendent of Abraham, Isaac, and Jacob. I am one of God's people and a part of His church. *Israel*. He *wants* me to wrestle with Him, to fight for Him, to grapple with the Mystery, to hold on tight and refuse to let go. So much of my struggle has been about the struggle itself, feeling that faith should be easier, that encountering God should be a walk in the garden, not ten rounds in the ring. I've always known I was supposed to be a God believer, a God follower, a God lover, even a God proclaimer. But I did not know I could be—*should* be—a God wrestler.

Thanks be to Jesus, my life *has* been a walk in the garden more often than I deserve. But thanks be to Yahweh, even through long, desperate nights on the Jabbok River—bewildering seasons of pain and doubt and exhausting struggle—I have sensed deep inside that I was held by the only arms that could bless me. I knew that seven years ago when I wrote this book, and I know it more so now. Like Jacob, I can resist God all night long if I want to. I can try anything else—grasping, scheming, deceiving, achieving—first. But like Jacob, I cannot be blessed until my own strength is overcome, until I end up hanging on for dear life and croaking out the same hoarse whisper of a prayer:

I will not let You go unless You bless me.

That's what this book is about. Thanks for reading it. May you find not only something of yourself, but also something of the God of Abraham, Isaac, and Jacob in these pages.

Carolyn Arends

Prelude

You hem me in—behind and before; you have laid your hand upon me. Such knowledge is too wonderful for me, too lofty for me to attain.

Psalm 139:5-6

1

Shoes

(it's the one I don't think it is)

I am five-and-three-quarters years old, and I'm under a lot of pressure. I am trapped in that claustrophobic space we kindergartners call the "Cloakroom"—an area carved out behind the blackboards for hats, coats, shoes, and the sweaty children who must wrestle them on. It is the end of the day, and once I have accomplished the supposedly simple task of putting on my outside clothes, I'm free to leave this murky place and head for the glorious freedom of the schoolyard.

It's the shoes that are giving me trouble.

The air is thick with chalk dust and fear. I am staring at my sneakers. It's not that I don't know how to tie them—I've been proudly demonstrating my ability to produce double rabbit's ears for months. It's just that I'm encountering some difficulty distinguishing my left foot from my right. It would be far too humiliating to ask my teacher, the ironically named Mrs. Shoemay, for help. I know I can do it myself.

But the shoes are just lying there, maddeningly similar to one another. And the clock is ticking. Most of my classmates have left, fully and properly clothed.

Weeks of this daily ordeal have forced me to develop a system, one that has evolved through trial and excessive error. I repeat this simple yet cunning mantra under my breath: "It's the one you don't think it is."

Experience has taught me that in almost all cases, I choose the wrong shoe first. But applying this wisdom is difficult. I decide to start with my left foot.

I focus in on a shoe. I'm pretty sure it's the left.

Aha! If my instincts tell me this is the left shoe, then it must really be the other sneaker I need.

I set my sights on the other sneaker. It's definitely the left. Why didn't I see it before?

But wait. If I think that's the one, then of course it's the other shoe—the one I don't think it is. OK. But now that I think it's *this* one, it must be *that* one. Which means it's really *this* one...

I stare at my shoes through increasingly tearful eyes, lost in this hopeless game of mental tetherball, until pity (or frustration) drives Mrs. Shoemay into action. She finally slips the correct shoe onto my left foot, and I sigh knowingly.

It's always the one I don't think it is.

I am filled with a longing to be older, to know with a Mrs. Shoemay-like certainty my left foot from my right. I am yearning for the day I don't sometimes print my *b*s as *d*s and, also, it would be nice to cross the street by myself. I can hardly wait to be the Grown-Up, and when I close my eyes I can picture myself smiling a gentle but confident smile, listening to some hapless child's endless questions, and patiently responding with all of the answers.

Except that already, in my darkest and scariest moments, I have found myself wondering for just a crazy, precarious fraction of a second if maybe there's an answer or two the Grown-Ups don't actually know. I reject this heretical notion the second I think it, squeezing my eyes and fists until it's gone. But there remains a vague uneasiness I can't banish completely.

Ever since the pastor's wife taught her cheery Sunday school lesson on heaven, I have been troubled by the concept of Eternity. "God has always been," she told us in her happiest voice, "and He will always be. Like the rim of this glass. We can't see where the circle begins or ends." I didn't put up my hand when she asked if we had questions. I was a dutiful participant during Coloring Time, taking extra care not to make the Streets of Gold glitter outside the lines. But now there are nights when I lie in my bed, staring at the purple-fringed canopy above me (I am the only girl in kindergarten with a canopy bed), and I think about circles with no beginning or end, and about God, and about living with Him forever. And I panic.

It's not that I don't believe in God, or heaven. As long as I've known even my own name—maybe before—I've known that Jesus loved me. And there was a time, at my Nana and Granddad's house—a whole year ago now—when I knelt down with my mom by the plastic-protected sofa and prayed with all my might that Jesus would come into my heart. And He did.

It's just that I can't make any sense of Eternity—of time never coming to an end. I wonder what we'll do for forever, and it makes me feel strange and uneasy to try to imagine it. It's not that I favor the alternative—I don't want my life, or my parents' or grandparents' or neighbors' lives, to suddenly stop someday. Heaven is definitely the better option. But when I think about Eternity I get the queasy feeling in the pit of my stomach that there are Really Big Things I don't know—not bad things, necessarily, just impossible-to-understand things. And I don't like it.

Twice now I have tiptoed to my parents' bedroom and crawled under the covers with them, waiting for the smell and feel of them to calm me and slow my pounding heart. They have murmured sleepy reassurances and stroked my hair, and it has helped. I've been willing to overlook the fact that they really haven't explained Eternity to my satisfaction. I imagine they are waiting until I am a little older, a little better able to understand. Maybe once I'm six they'll feel I'm ready.

In another 24 hours I will sit in that miserable cloakroom wondering once more if I can trust my instincts. I will learn, of course, that I often cannot. My left sneaker will continue for at least a few more months to masquerade as my right, and it won't be the only thing in my life that isn't what it seems. Even when I finally am a Grown-Up (or at least a person old enough to impersonate one), I will sometimes turn right when I should go left. Even when I have been crossing streets by myself for years, I will occasionally cross the wrong street altogether. And even when I have my own child to reassure, I will lay in my bed and wonder about Eternity and demand answers I am not yet ready to understand.

But for now, Mrs. Shoemay has freed me, and outside in the sunlight, my mom is waiting. She'll take my hand, and we'll cross Porter Street together, and she'll tell me more of what she knows about shoes and streets and cars and the sun and the moon and the Jesus who lives in my heart.

Reaching

There's a time I can recall
Four years old and three feet tall
Trying to touch the stars and the cookie jar
And both were out of reach
And later on in my high school
It seemed to me a little cruel
How the right words to say always seemed to stay
Just out of reach
Well I should not have thought it strange
That growing causes growing pains
Cause the more we learn the more we know
We don't know anything
But still it seems a tragic fate
Living with this quiet ache
The constant strain for what remains
Just out of reach

We are reaching for the future, we are reaching for the past
And no matter what we have we reach for more
We are desperate to discover what is just beyond our grasp
But maybe that's what heaven is for

There are times I can't forget
Dressed up in my Sunday best
Trying not to squirm and to maybe learn
A bit of what the preacher preached
And later lying in the dark

I felt a stirring in my heart
And though I longed to see what could not be seen
I still believed
I guess I shouldn't think it odd
Until we see the face of God
The yearning deep within us tells us
There's more to come
So when we taste of the Divine
It leaves us hungry every time
For one more taste of what awaits
When heaven's gates are reached

We are reaching for the future, we are reaching for the past
And no matter what we have we reach for more
We are desperate to discover what is just beyond our grasp
But maybe that's what heaven is for
I believe that's what heaven is for

There's a time I can recall
Four years old and three feet tall
Trying to touch the stars and the cookie jar
And both were out of reach[1]

2

The Letter

(an explanation of sorts)

Let me start by displaying my gift for the obvious: I've decided to write a book. What is less obvious is what would possess me to do such a thing. While I am certainly a passionate lover of books, it has never been my duty nor my presumption to actually try to create them. I've always had the release valve of music to deal with any thought or emotion I just couldn't keep to myself, and I've been perfectly happy with my vocational life as a recording artist. So why on earth would I embark on the excruciatingly vulnerable task of committing to paper little bits of my life, subjecting myself to the deflating process of reducing the sum total of my experience to a series of ordinary words?

It all started, innocently enough, with a letter. Or rather, a request for a letter.

Upon the completion of my third album—a project I had somewhat ironically entitled *This Much I Understand*—I received a call from Matt, the record company publicist. "Just write a quick note explaining where your new album is coming from," he said. "It will be great." Publicists use the words "quick" and "great" a lot, and I knew such a letter was likely to be neither of those things. But Matt's exuberance blurred my thinking, and I agreed to deliver a note within a couple of days.

My albums consist of my songs, and my songs consist of my life, and my life consists of…well, presently, diapers and chaos and something I'm going to refer to vaguely as a lack of clarity. So writing about the album in question with any degree of coherency proved to be a challenge. I tried all my usual creative disciplines: prayer, contemplation, mindless television viewing, and copious amounts of chocolate. Nothing worked. Suddenly anything other than the task at hand became fascinating and relentlessly urgent, including, but not limited to, sorting photographs from the 1970s and reading the ingredients on the backs of shampoo bottles. Matt began to send enthusiastic emails asking when he might expect my quick, great note. I ran out of chocolate.

Around this time my infant son was still waking regularly every night, and I blamed my inertia on sleep deprivation.

Finally, in the wee and weakened hours of another predawn, I collapsed at the computer and decided to at least document the fact that I had nothing to say. I was too tired to engage in my usual editing procedures (which typically consist of asking myself "why in heaven's name did you write *that*?" and hitting the delete key). I just typed. And in the morning I sent a letter to Matt.

I had a friend who was rich but didn't own much—a guitar, some books, and a road-weary Jeep. That Jeep took a spill on a moonlit stretch of highway and, without so much as a "see you later," my friend was out of here. Now this friend was a nomad—a restless soul who never could seem to settle down—and when he left I knew he had finally found his home. But I wasn't so sure we could spare him. His death hit me like a bucket of ice water and left me startled and shivering and mad as a wet hen. But awake. Definitely awake.

I never got to tell my friend that I had a secret—a happy secret I couldn't hide much longer: I was sharing my personal space with a person-in-progress. My road band started tolerating more bathroom breaks and my husband painted the spare room a gender-neutral green and blue. We bought baby books and worried and laughed and tried to imagine our love personified.

My son made his debut on my own thirtieth birthday—talk about your milestones. I don't know if any of us were ready—it took a long time to coax him out into the world. But at last he arrived, covered with the evidence of his arduous journey, a beautiful, perfect, holy mess. We named him Benjamin and they let us keep him. He lives with us but he's not from around here. Every time we check, he still has the fingerprints of God all over him.

So there I was—unwillingly awakened by my friend's departure, physically wounded from a difficult labor, dizzy with love for the nine-pound miracle in my arms. It seemed like as good a time as any to make a record.

I heard about a studio on an island off the coast of Vancouver—a place where I could work and fish and stare at the stars you can't see in a city sky. We lived there for a summer, changing guitar strings and diapers and ourselves.

But the task at hand was daunting. I had to somehow take all the emotion and epiphany and confusion swimming in my head and harness it into a few three-and-a-half-minute songs. Lyrics and melody have always been my meditation, therapy, and education, and they have often been my prayer. But I was writing with a new urgency. Not only was I struggling to figure out what I wanted to say to myself and to the friends who listen to my music, now I was sorting out what I wanted to tell my son. And suddenly how little I understand—about everything—was vividly apparent to me.

I was coming up with a mass of contradictions. Life is short—don't waste a minute of it. Life is long—don't rush it. Life is cruel—watch your back. Life is beautiful—open your heart. I kept looking for the cohesive overview, a way to organize each of my observations into a neat outline. But if one exists, I didn't find it. Life is messy. Life is mystery.

"If you want mess and mystery," said a wise friend, "read Psalms." There I found not resolution, but revelation.

The LORD will watch over your coming and going both now and forevermore. Psalm 121:8

And so I wrote about the cruel, short, beautiful, long adventure that is this life. I wrote about our coming into this world, and our going out of it, and about what happens in between. And it dawned on me that as much as my son was made to come into this world, we are all meant to go into the next one.

I hope that someday, when my son has done some living and wondering of his own, he can pull out this little record I've made and hear what I wanted him to hear—that this life is worth living because of the God who made it. A God who—if we look for Him at all—will keep surprising us with His presence in the midst of the craziness we've made of this world. He is the One who gathered my friend into His arms, and He is the One who placed Benjamin into mine. He is good. He is love.

This much I understand.

Matt said the letter was "great." He included it in some of the promotional materials for the album and posted it on the company Website. I returned to my previously scheduled neurosis—worrying about what people would think of the new album.

The recording was released, and people seemed to like

it and not like it in the usual percentages—no real surprises. Except that I started getting letters about the letter. My confession of the tension I felt between hope and confusion seemed to strike a chord with an unexpected variety of kindred souls, especially the ones who were on intimate terms with tragedy and grief. One evening I was participating in a live chat on the Internet set up to promote the album, and a man who identified himself as "Pastor Bill" from Colorado, typed the following message:

> Thanks so much for the "open letter"...I used it in our prayer meeting last Wednesday as I spoke about the [very recent] Littleton shooting. It was a really powerful letter as we wrestled with life being messy and a mystery.

In three albums I had written and recorded 33 songs, most of which were chiefly concerned with expressing the things I thought I understood. But this admission of all the things I didn't understand was connecting with people in a new and oddly powerful way. Hearing from those people did a wonderful, life-giving thing for me—it told me I was not alone.

I began to conduct an experiment. I was a little bolder in conversations, more open about the incredibly lopsided ratio of questions to answers in my world. At first I was nervous, expecting whoever was listening to me to launch into a prophetic judgment along the lines of "O ye of little faith!" But more often than not I got empathetic nods of understanding. I started speaking less with the careful accent I had cultivated over years of traveling in churched circles and began to let my true voice be heard—even when it was hoarse from hollering into the void. Hardly anyone acted particularly surprised, and I began to realize the voices around me didn't sound all that different from my own. I had thought I was a Lone Ranger—fighting off the enemies of doubt and fear in my own private melodrama. I can't tell you what a relief it was to discover my struggle was neither unique nor isolated. However much I might be wandering in my Wild West of a desert, I had plenty of company.

The friend I wrote about in my letter—the one with the books and the Jeep—his name was Rich Mullins, and he was a recording artist like me. (It would be more accurate to say that he was the sort of recording artist I hope to one day grow up to be.) Rich once literally forced me to read *Orthodoxy* by G.K. Chesterton. I vividly remember him sitting across from me while I read the first chapter, craning his neck to see what page I was on, fidgeting in excitement and anticipation, hardly able to contain himself. I was rather self-consciously aware that he was studying my face, waiting for my reaction when I got to the good parts. Within the first few lines of chapter I, Chesterton explains that *Orthodoxy* was written as an answer to a critic who had challenged him to support his ideas and explain his philosophy. "It was perhaps an incautious suggestion," Chesterton says of the critic's challenge, "to make to a person only too ready to write books upon the feeblest provocation."[2] Rich waited impatiently for me to read that line and then roared it out loud—"only too ready to write books upon the feeblest provocation!"—and slapped his knee as he relished a favorite punch line.

I wish Rich was around right now to laugh at my current

situation. Heaven knows I'm no Chesterton, but it turns out much to my surprise that I too can be easily provoked into writing a book. The blame can be placed squarely upon all the incautious souls who have encouraged me to explore more deeply the mess and the mystery of my life and assured me their own lives are no less messy or cryptic. My plan is to fill these pages with stories about some of the things that have happened to me up until now, and my own conclusions or lack thereof as to what these things mean. I suspect there will be nothing particularly noble here—I should warn you from the outset that I am prone to respond to difficulties with fear, cowering, and considerable whimpering. You won't find anything especially original here, either—at best I will merely document my own faltering steps on a well-traveled path. This would be a much more exciting and dramatic book if just once I had been kidnapped by pirates or miraculously cured from some dreadful disease. But truth be told (and I certainly hope it will be), my life so far has consisted mostly of a series of seemingly routine moments, completely unremarkable except for the fact that the God of the Universe chooses to encode Himself in even the most mundane aspects of our lives.

I dare to hope that maybe you will recognize a bit of your own journey in these stories. And with a preposterous optimism I've come to recognize as faith, I presume to pray that something here will draw you deeper into the mystery of a God who far surpasses our understanding and yet—I do believe—stoops to dwell among us in love.

Every happening, great or small, is a parable whereby God speaks to us, and the art of life is to get the message.

Malcolm Muggeridge

The Summers of
My Discontent

Everything difficult indicates something more
than our theory of life yet embraces.

George MacDonald

3

An Ordinary Life

Mr. Stewart was my grade eight English teacher. He was funny and challenging and he actually liked students, so we liked him. We even paid attention to him a reasonable portion of the time. Except, of course, for the last few weeks of the school year. The District Board insisted that school be in session until the very end of June, a policy that was as inefficient as it was sadistic. As soon as the mercury crept high enough to force teachers to open classroom windows, a summer haze seeped in and hovered like a thick, warm blanket over every desk. The air—pungent with the aroma of thirteen-year-old boys too socially unaware to be concerned with showers after physical education classes—became unbreathable. The ensuing suffocation left students listless—eyes heavy, heads heavier. Resistance was futile and naps were taken. Not even a consummate educator like Mr. Stewart was any match for the month of June.

And that is why I—one of the most neurotically keen pupils to ever attend Como Lake Junior Secondary School—was unabashedly yawning and staring wistfully out the window, completely indifferent to Mr. Stewart's attempts to engage us. He had abandoned his lesson plan 30 minutes earlier and was now relaying a story about an old college friend. I forget how it came up, but I imagine it had something to do with some piece of literature we were allegedly studying. Like the rest of my classmates, I was not physically able to care. And then, out of the hot blue sky, Mr. Stewart said something that broke my summer spell like an icy blast from a garden hose. While my fellow students remained in their stupors, I snapped to attention and shook my head in groggy amazement. Mr. Stewart had been describing his old schoolmate as "the most normal, typical guy imaginable, from the most conservative background possible," when he suddenly remembered a piece of evidence that would both illustrate and prove his point. "I mean, good grief," he laughed, "his dad was a banker and his mother was a nurse."

You can imagine my shock, particularly if I tell you that *my* father was a banker just as surely as *my* mother was a nurse. Up until that moment their occupations had certainly seemed sufficiently exotic to me. But something in Mr. Stewart's monologue triggered a rare, lucid moment of self-realization, and I saw the truth. I was from an utterly normal, conservative background. I was horrified.

I guess I should have realized it sooner. After all, our family of five almost always held hands to say grace around meals of pork chops and applesauce, macaroni and cheese, or meat loaf. We took summer trips in a blue four-door Impala to places like Disneyland and the Grand Canyon. Every Monday night, my mother and I hunkered down with popcorn and Kleenex on the overstuffed couch and watched *Little House on the Prairie*. We had *The Sound of Music* soundtrack on vinyl. The evidence was irrefutable.

I had been writing songs and taking guitar lessons, and I was pretty sure that typical, conservative girls didn't become famous folk singers. I needed a dangerous, fascinating, or tragic background—something a biographer could at least call "interesting." But I had to face the facts. I lived in a middle-class house with a two-car garage and a welcome mat personalized with the family name. My banker father and my nurse mother fed and clothed my brothers and me, and they loved us well. There was no use in denying it, at least not while there was a bologna and Wonder Bread sandwich lurking under my desk in the lunch bag my mother had carefully packed for me that morning.

I don't know why it took Mr. Stewart's observation about his friend to reveal the obvious to me. Maybe I had been distracted by the weirdness that exists in even the most normal families. There was my father's sense of humor, for example. He might be revered in business circles, but he never once answered the question "What's for dinner?" with anything but the same maddening reply: "Chicken gizzards and lizard legs." When his frustrated offspring moved on impatiently to the inevitable follow-up question, there was again only one response.

"Seriously, Dad, where's Mom?"

"The last time I saw your mother, she was running down the street, tearing out her hair, screaming, 'Why won't my children clean their rooms?'"

In addition to my father's unique wit, there was also my mother's exuberance. She was large of heart, thin of skin, easily moved to both laughter and tears, and never particularly quiet about any of it. I can still remember lying in my crib listening to my mother's cheers carry down the hallway from the living room, her voice growing increasingly hoarse as she urged on the Vancouver Canucks as if the outcome of their entire hockey season hinged on her support. Such displays of enthusiasm merely foreshadowed the level of passion (and corresponding volume) she reached when her own children were old enough to take part in sporting events, piano recitals, and spelling bees.

Still, however quirky my parents might be, they were hopelessly regular about it. No amount of silly jokes or noisy public displays of parental pride could camouflage the essential normalcy of our family. And even if I had been able to convince an onlooker that we weren't so conservative after all, I would have been completely undone by the indisputable fact that—above all—we were religious.

Every Sunday morning we climbed into dresses and suits, jostled for position in the Impala, and filed into our usual pew—left side, five rows back—at Blue Mountain Baptist Church. (Years later I would hear an acquaintance describe the church of his own youth as "A-frame, organ on one side of the baptismal, piano on the other—you know, the classic Baptist design," and realize with a start that even my church's architecture was utterly typical.) My father was the organist, my mother was the children's choir director, and I was an enthusiastic youth group member who was already writing songs to go with the pastor's four point sermons. If I was looking for a dangerous, fascinating, or tragic background, I certainly wasn't going to find it in the orange-cushioned pews of Blue Mountain Baptist.

Persuaded by my own prosecution, I endured the rest of that hot June school day with a sinking heart, thoroughly convinced that my normal family and my conservative church had, by their love for me, condemned me to the monotonous prison of the ordinary. My conclusions seemed indisputable, and for the next several years I remained unaware of how completely idiotic they were.

It has taken me the better part of two decades to retry my case and to begin to understand that the ordinary is not only not a prison, it is not even ordinary—that every single breath inhaled by every fragile human in this colossal cosmos is an extraordinary phenomenon of the wildest proportions. It has also taken several forceful and, frankly, often unwelcome confrontations with the reality of things both seen and unseen to reveal to me what I should have known all along. My typical Baptist church—with its strange rituals of hymnody and communion and its outrageous claim that it was God's house and its people were His people—was the perfect place to uncover a story far more dangerous, tragic, and fascinating than I dared to imagine. I know now that there is very little about this life that can in any way be described as "normal." But if you had tried to tell me that in Mr. Stewart's eighth grade English class, you could not have convinced me. Some things have to be lived before they can be believed.

If we had a keen vision of all ordinary human life, it would be like hearing the grass grow or the squirrel's heart beat, and we should die of the roar that lives on the other side of silence.

George Eliot

The temptation is always to reduce life to size. A bowl of cherries. A rat race. Amino acids. Even to call it a mystery smacks of reductionism. It is *the* mystery.

Frederick Buechner

4

A Summer in the South

The summer of 1993 was uncharacteristically humid in Nashville. At least that's what the weathermen and gas station attendants all told us. Any summer we spent in Tennessee, the locals, by way of apology, claimed the heat was unusually bad (as if under more typical circumstances a refreshing ocean breeze was known to waft down the Cumberland River, keeping everything perfectly reasonable). In one sense they were telling the truth—it *was* abnormally hot and humid, at least for mild-climate Vancouverites like my husband and me. We always swore we would never come back in July or August, but we always did. Mark's job as a teacher gave us freedom in the summer months, and we were prone to a peculiar amnesia that made us forget just how hot it got in Tennessee until it was too late to come to our senses and beat a quick retreat back to the Pacific Ocean.

We arrived on the Fourth of July and hit the outskirts of Nashville just in time for the fireworks. We were flattered to receive such an extravagant welcome, but it was hard to keep our bleary eyes open. There are just over 2500 miles between Nashville and Vancouver, and we had driven them in three eighteen-hour days. We had seen most of America's midsection through the bug-stained windows of our little white Chevy. Now all we wanted to see was a bed.

We were cranky enough to honk a bit at the pickups and station wagons strewn leisurely across I-24. The drivers waved and honked enthusiastic replies, happy to have us join their party. There were bare arms and legs dangling from every window, whole families sprawled on blankets in the beds of trucks—no one was remotely interested in going anywhere. We had no choice but to pull over to the side of the road and watch the fireworks explode against the southern sky. The cacophony of competing radio stations blaring from neighboring vehicles made conversation impossible, so we reclined our bucket seats and grinned at each other, a couple of tired, crazy fools.

Aside from a nasty run-in with a ticket-wielding Missouri state trooper, we'd had a good trip, and we had spent much of it basking in the romantic, poetic light of our adventure. At 25 and 29, we could still (we hoped) be considered young, we were definitely in love, and if you squinted at our '89 Cavalier the right way you could almost be convinced that it was a sports car. It would have been a nice touch to have the wind blow through our hair, but for most of our journey it was too hot to open the windows, so we kept the air conditioner on "high" and achieved approximately the same effect. Now that we had almost reached our destination, the celebration— complete with pyrotechnics— seemed rather ridiculously perfect.

The fireworks finally sputtered out and the revelers began coaxing their engines back to life and meandering their way down the freeway. Mark inched us into traffic, and I returned to my duties as trip navigator and disc jockey, quickly checking the map and then turning my full attention to the infinitely more important task of scanning our box of compact discs for the right arrival music. I settled triumphantly on some geographically relevant Paul Simon.

> *I am following the river*
> *Down the highway*
> *Through the cradle of the Civil War*
> *I'm going to Graceland,*
> *Graceland*
> *In Memphis, Tennessee*
> *I'm going to Graceland*
> *...I've reason to believe we all will be received*
> *In Graceland*[3]

Strictly speaking, we were actually going to stay with some friends in Franklin (just south of Nashville), not Memphis, but the song still seemed to fit. We played it over and over again until we pulled at long last into the driveway of our hosts' house and staggered, still humming the chorus, towards a good night's sleep.

It was not hard to remember that we were in the cradle of the Civil War when we stayed with Chris and Sally Jones. Our friends themselves were transplants—Sal was from Alberta, Chris was from New York—but if their creaky house's 100-year-old walls could talk, they would undoubtedly speak in a genteel southern drawl. After all, you couldn't throw a rock over the Jones' backyard fence without hitting the grave of a confederate soldier. The whole place seemed to rustle with history, animated by—not ghosts, exactly—but a palpable sense of other times and other lives.

The house was also animated by, well, animals. Mark and I were only two of the many strays Sal took in. Dodee the Black Labrador we knew from previous visits, but Daisy the Golden Retriever was a recent addition to the family, and three new cats had joined the menagerie. One of them—Chessie—came with the house, and whatever history she carried around with her had left her more than a little paranoid. Whenever we encountered her in the hallway, there was an awkward, cagey pause before she took great pains to step around us, her coal-black fur bristling at the outrage of our intrusion.

I wasn't really a cat person, anyway. Truth be told, I was almost afraid of them. Growing up, my father's allergies had made our household rather hostile to any feline presence. I would take a big, slobbering hound any day over an aloof, disdainful feline. Cats as a species were far too secretive, and I always had the feeling they were barely tolerating me.

Sally's cats must have smelled my fear. Chessie kept her wary distance, but the other two creatures sought me out day and especially night. In the wee hours they would creep into the guest room and slink onto the bed. Inevitably, both cats would settle on my chest and spend the rest of the night relentlessly kneading my rib cage with their paws. Even their purrs of contentment seemed a little menacing in the dark, their pleasure rattling in their chests like the rumble of distant thunder. I was having trouble sleeping.

I don't know what it was, exactly—perhaps the oppression of the heat or of the cats, the lack of sleep or the absence of anything familiar—but I began to get a strange, alarming sense that all was not well. I tried for several days to shake it off or explain it away as fatigue or indigestion— I kept impatiently reminding myself that the feeling made no sense. We had come to the South for the express purpose of nurturing my dreams as a singer and a songwriter, and it seemed as if the dreams might actually be coming true. My days were happily hectic, crammed full with recording sessions, synergistic collaborations with other writers, and appointments with record company executives who were beginning to show tangible interest in my potential as a recording artist. It was an exciting time. But every night I would lie tense and disquieted, my brain buzzing ominously like the cats.

To this day, I remain almost completely baffled by what happened next. The vague and cloudy sense of foreboding began to take a more definite shape, until in the middle of one particularly sweltering night the walls of our little guest room closed in like a coffin and I lay trapped in a sweaty panic. Everything sane and solid and good in my life, everything I had believed effortlessly (instinctually and spontaneously, so that my believing was as natural as breathing), seemed all at once to disintegrate into absolutely nothing. Physically, I felt sick to my stomach, heart racing, fists clenched. Emotionally, maybe even spiritually, I was in cardiac arrest. The life-giving oxygen of faith and hope that had always sustained me was suddenly, inexplicably cut off.

I could not feel the presence of God.

I had said many times up until that moment that I simply could not understand how a human being could rise every day with the sun, could hear Bach or the Beatles, could hold a squirming newborn or taste double-fudge ice cream or participate in any of the infinite number of small and persistent miracles of this life, and not believe in God. The idea that any living soul could be blind and deaf and numb to His obvious, insistent presence had always been unfathomable to me. Certainly I knew what it was to doubt—I had wrestled with the apparent contradictions I had encountered in Scripture, in my church, in my own nature. I had played the requisite mind games from time to time. *What if my faith in God is an inherited delusion? What if He is nothing like we think? What if He does not exist at all?* But however brave I felt I was being, however adrenaline-producing it was to stare down the barrel of my own mental pistol, it had always been a game of Russian roulette in which the gun was not loaded. That doubt had been intellectual (doubt of the mind), rather than visceral (doubt felt in the gut, the cellular tissue, and the soul). However dark it might occasionally seem without and within, there had always been a place deeper inside where a little light flickered away resolutely. I believed. I always had. And I thought I always would, until that stifling night in Franklin, Tennessee, when the air grew too thin to sustain the flame, and—in a perfectly still, awful instant—the light went out.

In the ensuing years I have remembered that moment sharply and distinctly, with a mixture of bewilderment and shame, and I have discussed it with hardly anyone. The times I have whispered it to a few trusted confidants, my confessions have provoked wildly disparate explanations. "Obviously," said my friend the Spiritual Warrior, "you were under attack. You were on the brink of entering into your ministry as a Christian artist, and the enemy was using the most devastating weapon in his arsenal to take you down." This interpretation seemed watertight until I spoke with my friend the Christian Mystic, who nodded knowingly. "Ah," he said, "the dark night of the soul. The cloud of unknowing. God reserves such tests of faith for the ones He loves best, the saints He trusts. You were on the brink of entering into your ministry as a Christian artist, and you were being refined, purified for the task." There were other friends with other hypotheses (including the Realist, who suggested that maybe I should just get over it), but almost all the interpretations could be traced back to one of these two antithetical views of doubt—doubt as an enemy to faith, or doubt as faith's refining fire. For much of my spiritual journey I have wrestled with and vacillated between these opposing theories. But that July night in 1993, I had no theories at all. I had only fear, and sadness, and the desolation of an unspeakable emptiness.

By morning I had fought my way to an extremely fragile equilibrium, pulling myself together enough to function normally at the breakfast table. No one seemed to notice that anything was awry, although the cats were looking at me rather suspiciously. I bowed my head—ostensibly to silently bless my French toast—and made a solemn vow: If I could no longer believe as a natural reflex of the heart, I would believe as a conscious exercise of the will. Looking back, this response was probably less a virtuous commitment to faith and more about self-preservation—even in the midst of my crisis of uncertainty I knew that more than anything else I did not want to inhabit a godless universe. Whatever my motivation, I was somewhat grimly resolved to strain towards, rather than away from, belief.

My Nashville schedule remained frantic, and I was grateful for the distraction. The storm inside my soul settled down to a dull roar, and sometimes I was almost able to convince myself that nothing was wrong. But there were so many questions lurking just below the surface. I would sit down with Mark, Chris, and Sal to watch the evening news—perfectly-coiffed and tanned anchors cheerfully reciting the day's tragedies—and find myself overwhelmingly disturbed by the problem of pain in the world, the suffering of innocents, the injustice that universally characterizes human experience. I understood the concept of free will, and yet I knew also that there were times God chose to supernaturally intervene—so why would He choose *not* to intervene in cases where, say, a child was forced to endure the horror of war, or cancer, or an abusive home? I had certainly pondered this question before, but now it had progressed from a riddle to a threat. I would open my Bible, hoping against hope that I would find comfort and certainty in the pages, and instead I would find myself bewildered by an apparently angry and alien Old Testament God who seemed only too willing to smite a whole nation of men and women and innocent children to prove a point. Or I would just hold my Bible to my chest, trying with all my might to recapture the confidence I used to feel in the men who had written and assembled it, wondering how I could have been so unwaveringly certain that they had gotten it right.

That certainty was what I mourned the most. Growing up in the North American evangelical culture of the 1970s and 1980s—where all the sermon points started with the same letter or formed an acronym, and the enigmas of redemption and sanctification were demystified into three or four easy steps—I had somehow absorbed or manufactured the idea that if I was a strong enough Christian, God and His interaction with the world and His children would make consistent sense to me. With complete sincerity I had embraced a sort of sitcom spirituality, in which all those gloomy trials and sufferings the apostles insisted on mentioning were viewed strictly as foils for inevitable victories—fleeting problems to be dramatically, swiftly, and neatly resolved, preferably within one thirty-minute episode. I was raised on stories of the great moments of the faith, from the parting of the Red Sea to the arrival of the Israelites in the Promised Land. We had tended not to dwell on the forty years of wilderness in between.

On some level I must have known that there was bound to come some trouble, but I expected it to be an attack from the outside—financial problems, failing health, spiritual persecution. I never once anticipated an uprising from within—a troubled intellect, a questioning heart, a desolate soul. I had gravely underestimated the scope and intensity of the condition I had once heard a friend call the Divine Frustration—the strain endured by any finite crea- ture who seeks to know and love an infinite Creator. I knew about the faithfulness of God, the tenderness of God, and the righteousness of God. But now I was encountering the mystery of God, and frankly, I didn't much care for it. The strain seemed more than I could manage.

Hindsight has not completely illuminated that dark summer for me, but now I can at least see that part of the ter- ror I felt was rooted in my unconscious belief that it was heretical to not be certain about every aspect of God. I don't know if I would have articulated it that way—I probably would have paid lip service to the idea that God is bigger than our comprehension—but at my core I was not prepared for all the paradox that was beginning to mark my encounters with

Him. Pinned beneath the cats in the Jones' guest room, peering tensely into the dark, I suddenly found myself staring into the gaping chasm of the infinite number of things I did not—could not—understand. I was left questioning everything—especially my right to question anything—and I could not shake the uneasy feeling that, in the words of my Southern friends, I didn't know "come here" from "sic 'em."

I could not make a mental distinction between my image of God (and my beliefs about God) and God Himself. So when I began to question my belief system, it felt like I was challenging God—and that was the one thing my belief system could not allow. I'd had enough truly life-changing encounters with God that it devastated me to think I might be turning my back on Him or letting Him down. And so hanging over even the lightest and brightest moments of that summer was a dark, brooding storm cloud —the sense not only of betrayal but of being a traitor.

I went about my business and, oddly enough, it was a productive time. We went to concerts and movies, caught up with our Nashville friends, and, of course, complained about the heat. Life went on, much as it had before, except that now I was constantly praying a singular, desperate prayer:

Please, God, please, make it like it used to be.

My idea of God is not a Divine Idea. It has to be shattered time after time. He shatters it Himself. He is the great iconoclast. Could we not almost say that this shattering is one of the marks of His presence?

C.S. Lewis

5

The Journey Home

We didn't take a lot of photographs that summer. We were too busy, and I was a little too morose. But Mark insisted on documenting a particular landmark on the way home, and I still have the snapshot. I am in the picture, and I am laughing. It is debatable whether the laughter is joyful or maniacal—suffice it to say I am laughing hard. My hair was longer then, and in the shot it is twisted and splayed like a wind-whipped flag. I am leaning with pointed significance against the very skinny pole of an unassuming roadside placard that could easily be overlooked in the shadow of the much larger, self-important "Food and Lodging 5 Miles" sign a yard or two before it. The little sign stands forlorn and noble, ringed in an equally pitiful patch of withered grass, fulfilling its humble destiny by marking what should be a creek, but is currently only a parched creek bed. The sign says, in tiny white letters, "Crazy Woman Creek."

I love the photograph because it makes me hopeful that I was not a completely sullen traveling companion—that there was at least a little levity during the 54-hour trek back to Vancouver. Surely I must have taken the odd coffee break from myself and the drudgery of my thoughts—otherwise I would never have managed so spontaneous an act as jumping out of the car on the precarious edge of Highway 70 to grin psychotically for the camera. Considering I never did find an "I stared into the abyss and all I got was this lousy T-shirt" souvenir, the photograph is the best memento I have of that difficult summer—a full-color illustration of a time when I was a woman as crazy and dry as the pebbly remains of Crazy Woman Creek.

We drove back the way we came, and for most of the first two days our Chevy hurtled like the Batmobile along Highway 70, all the way from St. Louis to the center of Utah. Kansas—which was somewhere in the middle—was even flatter than we remembered it, and we liked it that way. Mark discovered that in the long, straight stretches he could steer with his knees, dig out a well-worn deck of cards, and beat me soundly and repeatedly in games of Gin Rummy and Hearts. I never won. My heart wasn't in it.

I don't remember much of those first two days. I slept

a lot. I've always had vehicular narcolepsy—the steady hum of a car, train, or plane engine typically lulls me into a hypnotic sleep within minutes. Mark was patient and sweet, letting me doze, and he only complained a little when I woke up occasionally to ask him to stop for more Diet Coke or (30 miles later) a restroom.

My memory is oddly selective, so I've had to ask Mark what he recalls of that journey back across the wide-open spaces of America. He tells me that somewhere near Topeka, under cover of the dark of the first night, I began to haltingly speak more openly about my crisis of faith. He even has a vague memory of putting forth his own tentative, newly developing theory that God's truth was more expansive than we had previously imagined, and that maybe it was just possible that part of the reason I was feeling so fractured was that God was forcing His way out of the box we'd been keeping Him in. Apparently I burst into tears, terrified my husband was turning into a Make-Up-Your-Own-God Universalist, or, even worse, that he was almost as wretchedly uncertain about everything as I was. He tells me that between my sobs I managed to choke out something along the lines of, "Then we don't even know the same God!" I personally have no recollection of that particular conversation. (Some memories are better left suppressed.)

There is one memory, however, that Mark and I don't have to coax each other to recall. As the sun was setting on the second day of our drive, we began to cut our way across Utah on Highway 15. We were still a few hours outside of Salt Lake City, and we were absentmindedly discussing how long we could wait before we needed to stop for dinner. I was feeling antsy—keenly aware of my continued misery—ready to crawl out of my own skin and be anywhere else. In need of a cool compress, I was leaning my feverish forehead against the air-conditioned glass of the passenger-side window, staring into space. And then it happened.

We found ourselves right in the middle of the canyons of Utah. We have since discovered that other people have heard of them, but at the time they caught us completely by surprise. On our trip down seven weeks earlier, we had hit this stretch of highway at night, in the rain, and we had seen nothing but the beams of our own headlights. But now the canyons were filling every window—golden red, incandescent, and chiseled into an infinite number of intricate, exquisite angles—a billion glimmering diamonds carved out of the stone. While we gaped the sun descended, no longer distant and aloof, drawing lower and closer to warm the ruby rocks—first into glowing embers, then into blazing fires, and finally bursting out in explosions of glory. It was so intensely brilliant we had to look away, but there was nowhere to turn. Before us and behind us and on every side, we were hemmed in by unbearable beauty.

Once again I was aware of a constriction in my chest, once again I could not breathe. I had spent an anguished summer cajoling and begging and commanding God to answer my questions, devastated by what I perceived to be His silence, and now all at once it seemed that even the rocks were crying out on His behalf. I became in that moment a sort of poor man's Job—infinitely less tried, immeasurably less true, but nonetheless able to see in a holy flash a little of what it must have been like for Job to stand awestruck, repentant, wildly joyful, and gravely humbled by the voice of God.

Where were you when I laid the earth's foundation? Tell me, if you understand. Who marked off its dimensions? Surely you know! Who stretched a measuring line across it? On what were its footings set, or who laid its cornerstone while the morning stars sang together and all the angels shouted for joy?[4]

Who shut up the sea behind doors when it burst forth from the womb, when I made the clouds its garment and wrapped it in thick darkness, when I fixed limits for it and set its doors and bars in place, when I said, This far you may come and no farther; here is where your proud waves halt?[5]

Can you bind the beautiful Pleiades? Can you loose the cords of Orion? Can you bring forth the constellations in their seasons or lead out the Bear with its cubs? Do you know the laws of the heavens? Can you set up God's dominion over the earth?[6]

Can you raise your voice to the clouds and cover yourself with a flood of water? Do you send the lightning bolts on their way? Do they report to you, Here we are? Who endowed the heart with wisdom or gave understanding to the mind? Who has the wisdom to count the

*clouds? Who can tip over the water jars of the heavens
when the dust becomes hard and the clouds of earth stick
together?*[7]

My own tears were a welcome rain—a desperately needed
watering of the sticky clouds of dust that had become my soul.
We drove silently through the canyons, as slowly as traffic
would allow, and even when the sun had set and the rocks were
shrouded in darkness, we could still feel their looming presence.
By the time we reached Salt Lake City, I was weary with wonder, and I laid my head on Mark's shoulder in an exhausted
acquiescence. I was praying—as deeply and directly as I've ever
prayed anything—a simple prayer.

Thank You.

And that is how, in the dusk of an otherwise unevent-
ful August day, my unanswered questions were answered
rather resoundingly with, well…unanswered questions. If I
could not understand how the world's foundation was laid, or
how the earth was suspended like a top in space, or how the
oceans and the clouds were dreamed into being and the stars
of a billion galaxies were flung across the sky—if I could not
hope to fathom these most rudimentary mysteries of the
physical world, how could I expect to grasp the deeper mysteries of the eternal world? I have heard God's words to Job
interpreted as an explosion of righteous anger, but I believe
they were spoken with the infinite tenderness of a patient
father who is searching for a way to explain the unexplainable

to his impetuous, beloved child. At least that is how the words were spoken to me.

We stopped somewhere on the edge of the city for cheeseburgers, and then we pointed our little, white, quasi-sports car north and west, leaving red-clay tread marks behind us in the diner parking lot. I was feeling shattered and whole and foolish and elated all at once. Around the time our headlights found the "Welcome to Idaho" sign, I was laughing out loud (Mark must have thought I had finally really cracked) at the realization that I had spent an entire miserable summer devastated by how little I could see when I tried to examine God through my own myopic microscope. I had expected to fully apprehend the Lord of the Universe on the basis of the perceptions of Him I had accumulated fumbling about on this planet. I would have had a better shot at extrapolating the canyons of Utah from a few fragments of ruddy rock.

We crashed in Boise, at a motel that AAA had rather generously given a rank of two stars. The room reeked of cherry-scented disinfectant, and the bed—which was slightly less comfortable than a sheet of plywood—was way too small for a girl and her 6'3" husband to share. But even crushed between my slumbering mate and the wall, I was breathing better than I had in weeks. There were no cats, for one thing, and there was a new sensation I can most accurately describe as peace. Around three in the morning, I realized with another laugh that it was a peace that was *supposed* to pass understanding. This revelation came as quite a shock—I didn't have to be able to explain or prove something in order for it to be true. My brain was racing as fast as my pulse—maybe, just maybe, the truest, most essential things were the least comprehensible. Maybe I did not have to confine my faith to what I understood.

To this day I still sometimes mourn the simplicity and certainty that evaporated in the heat of that sweltering summer. God never did answer my desperate plea to make my faith like it used to be. Once I entered a little way into the Mystery, there was no going back. I could no longer list all the things I did not understand about God as threats to my faith—instead, they became the primary evidence that God was, in fact, God…and that I was, in fact, not. The Divine Frustration was a terrible strain. But it was also an indication that something infinite really existed, something my finite three-and-a-half pounds of brain could only know in part, like peering through a dark glass at a reality too intense to be seen safely with the naked human eye. I was no longer forced to reduce God to something less than infinite, or exalt myself to something more than finite—I could just go ahead and endure the tension, sometimes experienced most naturally and painfully as doubt, and believe anyway. And here was the most radical part: I could believe not only in spite of, but also in some ways *because of*, my unanswered questions.

Years later, when I stumbled across Pascal's claim that "reason's last step is the recognition that there are an infinite number of things which are beyond it," the places where I first learned that most difficult and life-giving lesson instantly appeared before my mind's eye. Chris and Sally's cat-invaded guest room. Crazy Woman Creek. The impossibly red canyons of Utah. A cheap hotel room in Boise, Idaho. In these unlikely locations I discovered a new way of breathing, and believing.

In the fall of 1995 I returned to Salt Lake City on official business as a recording artist—the opening act for a tour featuring Rich Mullins and Ashley Cleveland. I decided at the last moment to deviate from my normal set list in order to sing a geographically relevant song I had written about the red rocks that were only a stone's throw away. Afterwards, a young couple dropped by the autograph table and asked me to describe the canyons Mark and I had seen. "You can't have been far from one of our favorite vistas," said the girl, with a secret smile, "a place called Angels Landing."

Angels Landing. I checked a map, and that really is the name of one of the clusters of canyons. It seems that I am not the only one who has heard the rocks cry out somewhere near Highway 15, and seen—if only for a moment—something of the Eternal glimmering there in the golden red clay.

It Has to Be You

I don't know quite who I am anymore
I don't know if that's normal or not
I don't know if I know You at all anymore
At least not in the way that I thought
But I know there are canyons in Utah
Red as fire, high as the sky
And they make me cry
'Cause I don't know one living soul
Who could carve out of stone such a view
So I know—it has to be You
It has to be You

There are days all of my faith slips away
There are days that I don't even care
There are days I find myself desperately praying
And still can't believe You are there
But the sun, it comes up every morning
Blazing glory, consuming the night
And it's quite a sight
'Cause I can't find one living mind
Who could make the sun shine ever new
So I know—it has to be You
It has to be You

Well if I've built my hopes on mirrors and smoke
If it's all been a dream from the start
Why then can't I deny the yearning inside
More real than the beat of my heart

There's a voice I cannot hear with my ears
There's a voice I can hear all the same
There's a voice that speaks in my dreams and my fears
It is endlessly calling my name
And on warm summer breezes it whispers
Rivers carry its soft lullaby
And it makes me cry
'Cause I don't know one other love
That would go to such lengths to break through
So I know—it has to be You
It has to be You[8]

Landmarks
and Ebenezers

Without air, cells die;

without stories, ourselves die.

Neil Postman

6

Of Samuel
and Scrooge

I consider those moments in Utah in the August of my twenty-sixth year to be some of the most transcendent and defining of my life. Yet when I sat down recently to write about them I was startled by how much of that summer I could not remember. I was forced to go sleuthing about my own gray matter—and search Mark and Chris and Sal and old photo albums for clues—just to recollect details that I thought at the time would be vividly with me forever. I guess I haven't told the story much over the years, and that, I fear, is my loss. There is a scene in the movie *Avalon* in which a young boy asks his grandfather why he insists on retelling the family stories over and over again. The old man explains, "If we don't remember, we will forget."

We recognize instinctively the value of remembering our stories. We each have our own set of personal favorites, and we trot them out at parties as a way of introducing ourselves and as a kind of shorthand to who we are. The stories I end up telling at social gatherings—especially the ones that my friends ask me to repeat to new acquaintances—are typically not particularly profound. I am asked to describe, for example, the time I was standing awkwardly at the first meeting of a college freshman Bible study until my roommate tugged at the leg of my sweatpants to get me to sit down—inadvertently pulling the sweats right off and leaving me still standing and pants-less. Or the time a high school boyfriend made me laugh while drinking a soda—resulting in a sudden, terrible surge of Coca Cola through both my nostrils. "Are you OK?" he kept asking, and the only reply I could manage was, "Just don't look at me!" I've got a thousand "embarrassing moments"—so do most of the people I meet—and the mutual exchange of these stories grants an instant intimacy, the kinship of shared experience. But even if all a story does is provoke a good belly laugh, it's worth telling.

All the grandiose and mundane and silly things that happen to us, the wonderful little epiphanies and the ugly little thoughts that cross our minds and change our hearts, the times when nothing much seems to happen at all except that we are sitting around becoming who we are—it all matters. And so, when we gather around campfires or kitchen tables and begin "Have I ever told you about the time..." we engage in a profoundly important human activity. We acknowledge our connection to each other. We learn to listen to the meaning encoded in the happenings of our lives. And we remember so that we won't forget. I like to think that our stories become Ebenezers of sorts—an idea I have borrowed from one of the strange and wonderful stories of the Old Testament.

Samuel, of First and Second fame, was not only a prophet of God, he was an expert rememberer. Maybe he was a prophet at least partly *because* he was so good at remembering what everybody else tended to forget. The Israelites, for example, kept forgetting God, and Samuel kept reminding them to remember, until finally, in a town called Mizpah, he got through to them. The people agreed to get rid of their foreign gods—Baals and Ashtoreths and who knows who else—and then, assuring Samuel of their repentance, they asked the prophet to plead their case before the true God they had neglected. They fasted and prayed, and—as if to symbolize the pouring out of their hearts—they drew water and spilled it out before the Lord in a rather poetic gesture not precedented or repeated anywhere else in the Old Testament. "We have sinned against the LORD,"[9] they cried, and reading the story one gets the sense they really were sorry that they had forgotten their covenant with God.

Meanwhile the Philistines got word that the people of Israel had gathered together in Mizpah and were engaging in water-pouring and crying and all sorts of eccentric activities. The Philistines liked nothing better than warring against and beating the Israelites—something they did often—so they headed over to Mizpah in gleeful anticipation. The Israelites must have been having a truly transcendent moment with God, because when they heard the Philistines coming, for once they did not revert to their usual habit of scrambling frantically after their idols. "Do not stop crying out to the LORD our God for us," they begged Samuel, "that he may rescue us from the hand of the Philistines."[10] Samuel sacrificed a lamb, and he kept on fervently crying out to the Lord on Israel's behalf.

While Samuel was busy handling the burnt offering, the Philistines came roaring up to Mizpah looking for a fight. "But that day," the narrator of 1 Samuel tells us matter-of-factly, "the LORD thundered with loud thunder against the Philistines and threw them into such a panic that they were routed before the Israelites."[11] It was a very big moment for Samuel and his people. Not only did God forgive them, He gave them victory over their archenemies, who had been routinely pounding them for years. It was the kind of thing you tell your grandkids about.

But Samuel had enough experience to know that even a great moment like the one they were having could and probably would be forgotten over time. So he decided to build a little monument to the whole event. He took a rock and placed it out in the battlefield, somewhere between Mizpah and the neighboring town of Shen. He named the rock "Ebenezer," and while my post-Dickens brain is reminded instantly and absurdly of the infamous Scrooge, the Israelites understood the name to mean "stone of help." "Thus far has the LORD helped us,"[12] Samuel said ceremoniously. I don't know how long that stone stayed in its place, but it's easy to imagine grandchildren touring it like a museum, rolling their eyes a little as they hear for the umpteenth time about the great day their fathers' fathers finally remembered God, and God remembered them, and the good-for-nothing Philistines at long last got what they deserved.

Many of the storytellers in the Bible make a special effort to designate remembering a sacred activity, and they are careful to point out that the people not only remember God, but that God remembers the people. In my translation of the Bible the word "remember" is used specifically and intentionally to describe holy moments when God went out of His way to express love and concern for one of His children. He *remembered* Noah after the flood, He *remembered* His covenant with Abraham, and when the thief on the cross begged, "Jesus, *remember* me when you come into your kingdom,"[13] Jesus promised him that He would.

Samuel himself was born because God remembered his mother, Hannah. Back in I Samuel I, Hannah had prayed with a bitter soul and a broken heart before the Lord. She was barren, which brought her great sorrow, and to make matters worse, her husband's other wife, Peninnah, kept taunting her about it. Elkanah, the husband, loved Hannah, but he was not the most sensitive guy in the world, and unfortunately there were not yet any copies circulating of *Men Are from Mars, Women Are from Venus.* "Hannah," he would ask obtusely, "why are you weeping? Why don't you eat? Why are you downhearted? Don't I mean more to you than ten sons?"[14] Hannah, not surprisingly, just kept crying, and after one particularly trying family pilgrimage to the temple she'd had enough of Peninnah's needling and Elkanah's comforting to drive her to her knees.

"O LORD Almighty," she prayed, "if you will only look upon your servant's misery and remember me, and not forget your servant but give her a son, then I will give him to the LORD for all the days of his life, and no razor will ever be used on his head."[15]

Eli, the priest on duty at the temple, mistook Hannah's emotional state for drunkenness, which must have seemed to her to be an appropriate ending to a very difficult, stressful day. Hannah explained passionately that she had consumed no wine or beer at all, but rather had been pouring out her soul to the Lord—praying out of her great anguish and grief. Evidently Eli felt like a jerk because he quickly changed his approach and sent Hannah off with a blessing, "Go in peace, and may the God of Israel grant you what you have asked of him."[16]

The storyteller of 1 Samuel wastes no time telling us what happened next. "Elkanah lay with Hannah his wife, and the LORD remembered her."[17] Simple as that. When God remembered Hannah, He gave her little Samuel, and when Hannah remembered God, she gave Him Samuel back. It makes sense that when Samuel grew up to be God's own long-haired prophet, he understood that you have to remember the things that happen—especially those moments when it becomes clear that God has remembered you—so you don't forget everything that matters.

I don't know if Charles Dickens was thinking of Samuel's stone of help when he dreamed up his Scrooge, but maybe the connection to old Ebenezer actually makes some sense. After all, Ebenezer's vision of the present and the future began with a visit from the ghost of his past. By reminding him who he used to be, his memories helped restore to him all the essential parts of his humanity that he had forgotten. And though *A Christmas Carol* ends on Christmas Day, it's easy to imagine Ebenezer Scrooge spending the rest of his life eagerly recounting the story of his strange Christmas Eve over and over again, remembering with each telling the way he was changed forever.

I am trying to remember the red rocks of Utah so that I don't forget what God whispered in the wind blowing across Highway 15. Looking back, I can see there have been other encounters with the Divine, other brushes with the Mystery—some of them long before that difficult summer of 1993, and many of them since. The stories of these moments are my Ebenezers, places in my past where I can stop and stand for a moment and say, "Thus far the Lord has helped me." When I get lost, and I can't remember who I am or where I come from, these memories become for me a sort of bread crumb trail, leading me back home to the God who is not only worth remembering, but who—remarkably—remembers me.

Only be careful, and watch yourselves closely so that you do not forget the things your eyes have seen or let them slip from your heart as long as you live. Teach them to your children, and to their children after them.

Deuteronomy 4:9

7

The Fish Pond

If for some mysterious reason you wanted to shoot a documentary about my life, and you had to set the entire film in one location, the obvious choice would be Blue Mountain Park. It was the official Jonat family park (Jonat is my maiden name, which you should know if you're making a documentary about me) from the time I was a toddler until we moved away just before my sixth birthday. We returned to the neighborhood—the prodigal family—when I was 12, and we have played happily in the sun-dappled shadows of its massive pine trees ever since.

If you wanted to show the progression of years you could start at the tennis courts in the middle of the park. Some awkward prepubescent girl could portray the early me, lunging at tennis balls as they ricochet wildly off the freshly laid asphalt. She would be fiercely competitive and hopelessly uncoordinated, and you could film her laughing and sweating and expending enormous effort—vainly attempting to beat a moustached actor portraying my father, or an outlandishly tall child playing the role of my brother Chris. Eventually, you could cut to a self-conscious 15- or 16-year-old. She would be sitting shyly against the chain-link fence—her braces glinting in the sun—admiring her boyfriend's displays of athleticism on the now pock-marked courts. And then, should you wish to depict the present day, I could of course play myself—still awkward and competitive, still perspiring and losing—only now the asphalt would be wrinkled and cracked and in desperate need of a face-lift, and the worthy opponent would be my husband. Maybe we could even look a little way into the future and shoot a scene in which I am actually defeating Mark. He is, after all, four years, two months, and seven days older than me—eventually that has to give me some sort of an edge.

Blue Mountain Park is roughly two blocks long and two blocks wide, and there is a small buffer of flower gardens (somehow miraculously maintained despite the ever-present threat of Nike-clad feet) between it and the incessant traffic on Blue Mountain Street. Right next to the street is the baseball diamond. Like all the locals, I felt rather Major League the day the Parks Board installed lights around the edges of the outfield, and for several years now there have been baseball and softball games both day and night. I have spent countless Saturdays squirming uncomfortably on the aluminum bleachers, eating red licorice, and screaming myself silly in support of my little brother, Cam, who—because he is adopted and therefore exempt from the Jonat athletic curse—is a great pitcher.

Adjacent to the ball field, on the back side of the snack stand and the public restrooms (which we use only under the most dire circumstances), is the kiddie park—a bark mulch nirvana for my son and Mark and me whenever any of us feels an overwhelming need to get out of the house. Ben loves this area with an ardent passion—the swings and slides and teeter-totters, the life-sized plastic horses he can ride bareback, the sand pit complete with pulley-operated miniature backhoes, and the log fort that (when he really wants to give his mother a heart attack) he can scale like a very short and reckless mountain climber. On sunny days the place writhes with exuberant young lives, and their guardians shuffle around the edges comparing notes. *How old is your little guy— two? Ah, he's smaller than my Jason, but Jason has always been huge, like his father.* The park is in the middle of an increasingly multicultural neighborhood, and so these conversations take place in every tongue—French, Mandarin, Hindi, Italian, and variously accented English—but everyone is fluent in the universal language of Parenthood. Children are the ultimate icebreakers, and except for the odd haggard mother or father having a particularly trying day, almost all of us spend our time grinning at our kids and at each other—feeling connected by our mutual membership in the Society of the Sleep Deprived and the Blessed.

Beyond the play area is a lush stretch of forest, and no trip to the park is complete without a wild scramble through the evergreens, alders, and cottonwoods—Benjamin in pursuit of any dog that will give chase, Mark and me in pursuit of Benjamin. The dirt paths are booby-trapped with tree roots, so inevitably one of us comes crashing to the ground, and, if the victim's elbows and knees are not too bloody, the next logical event is a family dog pile. At this point in the documentary you could cut to three giddy Arends lying on their backs—hair full of pine needles, shirts stuffed with leaves—drinking in sunshine and birdsong and the sweaty scent of each other. These woods loom large in my history—they were the site of two clumsy first kisses, one heart-crushing breakup, and countless whispered barings of the soul—but they are even more solidly a part of my present. To Benjamin the trees must seem a thousand feet tall, and he loves to squint up through their branches to spot—with uncontainable excitement—the celestial visitations of each crow and seagull and airplane that grace our airspace.

The far side of the woods opens out into a clearing, a stretch of reasonably level lawn perfectly suited for the throwing of Frisbees and the staging of three-legged races. Picnic tables are scattered around the periphery, making this location ideal for Sunday school picnics. The good people of Blue Mountain Baptist Church have been spending greasy Sunday afternoons eating Kentucky Fried Chicken here for dozens of years, and I have often been a part of the happy throng. For the purposes of the documentary, you could edit in a couple of the photographs I took after church one Sunday just last summer. There is a wide shot of the baseball diamond—boys skinning their knees and men pulling their muscles in an impromptu but impassioned game of softball. And in another picture there are half a dozen children, including a very drenched and delighted Ben, splashing about the water park (which, although I haven't even mentioned it yet, is fabulous) under the watchful eyes of Jennifer, Jackie, Elise, Christy, and Megan—the helpful older girls who sometimes mind the kids so the women can talk.

None of those kids (and only a few of the women) know that there used to be a fish pond over on the other side of the woods. It was replaced with the much more exciting water park long ago, sometime during the six-and-a-half years I was living too far away to protest. But Chris and I can both remember the pond distinctly. It was constructed with flat heavy stones and mortar, shaped like a sawed-off, above-ground swimming pool, and filled with endlessly fascinating orange and brown fish. Our mother must have taken us there dozens of times. But there is one particular visit that has become the stuff of family legend, and it is the most indelible of all my Blue Mountain Park memories.

I was four, maybe five at the oldest; Chris was two or three. It was the early '70s, so there was undoubtedly a good deal of polyester involved. My dad was at work; my mom was with us. We had played hard in the kiddie park, ran through the woods, chased a few stray tennis balls, and stopped by the snack stand for grape Popsicles. We were only a short trip to the fish pond away from a perfect day at the park.

When we arrived at the pond, we were the only three visitors, so we felt especially free to chat with the fish, sing them silly songs, and engage in various other eccentric Jonat rituals. But my mother noticed right away that something was wrong. "Look!" she gasped, with genuine horror. "There is litter in the fish pond." We realized with a shock that it was true—some unimaginably derelict individual had sullied the water with a candy wrapper. If my memory is accurate, the trash was from an Oh Henry! chocolate bar.

Without hesitating, my mother began to climb up the rocky side of the fish pond. "Children," she said, panting a little with the exertion, "when we see litter like this, we have a chance to make the world a better place." She was balancing on the edge of the pond, and each time she reached out to grab the wrapper, a mischievous breeze blew it just a little out of reach. "Cleaning up garbage is simple," she exclaimed virtuously, shifting positions to try to get closer to the offending item, "and yet it makes such a big difference." We were nodding encouragingly, fully in support of the initiative to make the world a better place for the fish. "Remember," said my mother triumphantly, just as she finally got a good hold of the wrapper and began to drag it out, "it's up to us to do the right thing!"

And then she fell in.

We were terrified. She was lying face down in the water, and she was shaking. "Mom!" cried Chris. The fish— who appeared to be quite agitated—were radiating out and away from her body in every direction. "Help!" I shouted. No one came. It seemed certain that our mother was about to drown in six inches of pond water.

We were as relieved as we were confused when she finally managed to roll over and it became apparent that she was shaking with—of all things—*laughter*. Her favorite orange and green rayon pantsuit was torn, and her beehive hairdo had collapsed inwardly, so that it looked like a water-filled flowerpot. She was bleeding from several different locations. And, inexplicably, she was still laughing with a mirth so pure it was contagious. Chris and I laughed, too, although we were a little bewildered and quite anxious to get our mother out of the fish pond.

After several failed attempts, she managed to hurl her wounded self back onto dry land. She rested and bled a few moments on the grass, and then she stood up, ceremoniously dropped the candy wrapper into the nearest trash receptacle, took each of her children by the hand, and limped bravely and soggily home—laughing all the way.

In 20-odd years of hanging around Blue Mountain Park—cheering in its bleachers, losing on its tennis courts, falling onto leaves and into love on its wooded paths, fellowshipping with various saints at its picnic tables, and chasing my son over every blessed green inch—I have learned a few things. Play hard. Watch for birds and airplanes and other miracles through the trees. Pick up litter. Try to make the world a better place. And if you should fall—if you should find yourself bloodied and looking and feeling ridiculous—don't forget to laugh.

I imagine that the hardest part of filming a documentary is getting the ending right, so here is what I suggest. While your camera slowly pans the two square blocks of grass and trees off Blue Mountain Street, I can add a bit of narration, a rough translation of one of the best secrets Blue Mountain Park has taught me.

Take everything seriously, except yourself.

That's it. Not exactly Oscar-worthy, is it? So maybe your documentary won't be winning any trophies. But ever since I fished my mother out of the fish pond and glimpsed this humble little truth, it has served me well. The smaller and therefore more ridiculous we let ourselves be, the bigger our world and the eternity beyond it can become. Perhaps it would be an overstatement to say that this is the beginning of knowledge—but if it is not chapter 1, it is at the very least the Preamble to the Introduction. Benjamin, three feet tall, gazing with sacred awe at the sky above his thousand-foot trees, can see from his vantage point something very close to the true reality of things—something his altogether too serious mother has a tendency to miss. It takes a good, hard fall over shoelaces or tree roots to bring me back to earth, to leave me laughing on a bed of leaves, gazing up at a world of wonders and—for once—really seeing it. Those are the moments I can't help but think that all the realists who keep insisting that life is no walk in the park, have just never found the right park.

Angels can fly because they take themselves lightly.

G.K. Chesterton

8

A
Prairie
Storm

The relatives on my father's side were farmers—hard-working, plain-spoken people who understood and loved the earth and harnessed its power through sweat and skill and faith. At least that is how I imagine them. I am prone to remember them in fits of romantic contemplation, during which I suspect something of their noble, earthy spirit lives on in me. In my more lucid moments I see clearly it does not. Even my beloved Blue Mountain Park (one of the few places I frequent that is remotely close to resembling a wide-open space) is a *city* park, set in a concrete frame, and I must confess that I am the poster girl for comfort-craving suburbanites everywhere. When I get close to the earth I so profess to love, it seems, well…dirty.

I was not without promise in my early childhood. No Fisher Price farm set was ever as beloved as mine, and for six futile birthdays in a row I asked passionately and expectantly for a pony, whom I planned to call "Black Beauty" and keep in my bedroom. I see further evidence of my proud ancestry in my son, who is so enamored with cows that he reaches heights of near-ecstasy in the dairy section of our local supermarket. "Moo!" he cries, oblivious to the chill, pointing to the pastoral scenes that adorn each and every milk carton with a fervor that would have made his Great-Great-Grandma Bittner most pleased.

I met my great-grandmother only once, when I was very young. My parents, in a sudden spasm of suburban guilt (at least we know where I get it from), decided it was time to embark on a pilgrimage to the family homestead. And so, in the summer of 1972, my brother Chris and I spent a wide-eyed week on the Bittner wheat farm in Yorkton, Saskatchewan.

A four year old possesses a mind's eye like a fun-house mirror; the shapes of everyone and everything are stretched to larger-than-life proportions. To this day I can play back my memories like scratchy pieces of stop-motion film.

The wheat is militant, standing at attention in uniform rows until a prairie wind spots me in the distance and decides to put on a show. Stalks higher than the Empire

State Building become Motown dancers, bending and swaying, swaying and bending for an awestruck audience of one.
My great-uncles are benevolent Goliaths with wide grins and
huge, leathery hands. At the end of the day they smell a little
like ripe fruit. Their own children are no longer children,
and yet when they enter the farmhouse they are once more
the dutiful sons of Grandma Bittner, who is all one could
hope for in a family matriarch. Eighty-five laborious years
have compromised her mobility (I picture her in a wheelchair—my parents tell me it was really just a kitchen chair
from which she seldom moved), but she is still a dominant
figure. I am a little afraid in her presence, but there is a soft-
ness beneath her severe strength. The Saskatchewan sun has
turned her a golden brown, and she is as kneaded and plump
as the fragrant loaves of bread cooling on her counters.

The Bittner wheat farm is pure magic, but I am not
purely happy. Even a four year old can tell when something
is amiss, and I am troubled when my uncles' open faces
cloud over. I strain to overhear and understand their conversations. *The crops are in trouble. No rain for months.* We hoist
Grandma Bittner into the car for a drive, and each field we
pass elicits the same response. *Too dry, too dry.* My heart sinks
further with every mournful shake of her heavy head. I've
never heard the word "drought" before, but I'm sure it's not
good.

In the cool of the evening my great-aunts and uncles
gather in the kitchen and bring my parents up to date on the
latest family gossip. Chris and I grow restless, so one night we
are permitted to sit by ourselves on the front porch. We are

sleepy and warm and somewhat intoxicated with our freedom, until all at once the universe begins to go horribly wrong.

A cloud of mosquitoes attack my brother. The air is thick with them, and they only want Chris. We are mutually hysterical, and the grown-ups come running in the kind of panic that leaves spilt teacups and crushed pastries in its wake. The family surrounds my brother, and he is as frightened by their flailing attempts to beat off the insects as he is by the mosquitoes themselves. Eventually they manage to get him inside, and the surviving mosquitoes fly off in a well-fed stupor. With the resiliency only a two year old can possess, Chris is happy once again, consoled by some chocolate and an ancient set of building blocks.

Now I am alone on the porch, still sweaty and jittery from my brother's ordeal. Before my heart rate can return to normal, a new onslaught is launched. But this time it is not mosquitoes.

The world is suddenly lit in a ghoulish white flash that scorches my eyes. A second later, all is consumed in darkness. The wind begins to howl, enraged to be losing a shouting match with a thunder that is more terrifying than anything I've ever heard or imagined. The rain the heavens have been hoarding is released with a savage vengeance, pelting the roof and slashing at the windows, drenching me instantly. Even the sturdy old farmhouse has turned against me, violently banging the screen door open and shut behind me. The lightning strikes again and again and again, illuminating the holy terror that is my first prairie storm.

My parents find me inside the farmhouse, sitting on the cellar stairs, my hands clamped over my ears in an effort to drown out the rattle of the rain crashing into the huge metal rainwater cistern next to me. I am nearly doubled over by my sobs. My father scoops me up and carries me into the safety of the kitchen. A flash of hot light illuminates my relatives for a moment—inexplicably, they are sitting together staring out the farmhouse windows with strangely calm smiles. "It's just a storm," they murmur. There is even some quiet, gentle laughter. I only cry harder. "Sweetheart," pleads my mom, "don't be afraid." I shake my head. I am afraid, but more than that I am sick with a guilt so crushing I can't speak under the weight of it. The family—both immediate and extended—is sympathetic, patient. They don't understand that the chaos outside is *all my fault*. "What is it? What is it?" they chorus. Several minutes pass before I summon the courage to confess my terrible secret.

"I…prayed…for…rain."

Now the laughter is not so quiet. There is even a little applause. "Oh, honey, the rain is wonderful," someone says. Before I can catch my breath the uncles are teasing me. Someone brings me some warm milk, and soon I can't keep my heavy eyes open, not even to watch the storm. "Hey, sweetheart," calls an uncle as my daddy carries me off to my room, "could you pray for some cash?"

In the morning I awake to the sounds of my uncles' hammers. They are repairing wind-damaged fences, and they are still laughing, jubilant in the mud. The crops will make it after all.

The storm and the terror, the giddy relief and elation, the instinctual and unwavering belief that my prayer had saved the Bittner family farm—these are among my earliest memories. And I consider them now with a sense of both wonder and dread that has only deepened over the years. The night the Prairie Drought of 1972 came to an end was the night I began to understand that there are forces even towering great-uncles cannot tame, forces so ferocious in their power that—even if they bring you exactly what you need (*especially* if they bring you exactly what you need)—they are likely to scare you silly. I had already heard much about God in my young life—already, I think, learned to love Him. But hearing the heavens thunder I had my first taste of what it is to fear Him, my first encounter with what a quarter of a century later I am learning to call the *mysterium tremendum et fascinans*—the tremendous and fascinating mystery of God. On the front steps of that Yorkton farmhouse, a holy secret was whispered into my soul: Prayer is the point of access, the place where the finite and the infinite intersect and converse. To pray is to enter at least a little way into the Mystery, or—and this is even more dangerous—to invite the Mystery to come to you.

I have prayed every day of the 27 years since that stormy night, and yet it is only lately that I have become enough of a disciple to begin to study prayer—to stand with others and say, "Lord, teach me to pray." I recently devoured

Richard Foster's incredible book *Prayer: Finding the Heart's True Home*, startled to discover how many kinds of prayers are part of the Christian tradition—the Prayer of the Forsaken, the Prayer of Examen, the Prayer of Tears, the Prayer of Relinquishment, Meditative Prayer, Contemplative Prayer, Petitionary Prayer, Intercessory Prayer, Radical Prayer, and a dozen more. I have prayed many types of prayers throughout my life, but my haphazard list is quite different from Foster's.

I have been a specialist in the "Let's Make a Deal" school of prayer: *If You will only let me pass this test (for which I have not read the textbook), I will spend the rest of my life earnestly studying in a convent.* My years of frequent travel have also honed my "Turbulence Prayers." Typically whispered on airplanes that appear destined to crash, these prayers focus upon achieving meet-my-Maker readiness: *God, if there's anything not right between us, I confess it now.* I can also claim extensive experience with "Futility Prayers"—prayers that seldom work but are prayed passionately anyway. *Please make my newborn sleep through at least part of the night,* is one Futility Prayer; another is *Please don't let me throw up.*

However theologically incorrect my prayers may be, I have discovered that whatever is in my heart must be either prayed out or left to fester. And so I dare to utter my petty, self-interested requests, trusting—praying—that the Holy Spirit will intercede on my behalf with groans my words (or lack thereof) cannot express, translating my impetuous, childish gibberish into communion with God.

When I read that if I ask God for bread He will not give me a stone, I realize that He not only desires to give me what

I need, He wants me to come ask Him for it. This to me is the greater miracle, the deeper Mystery—the God of the Universe wants me to speak with Him. Heaven knows I am not a great conversationalist—I talk too much, listen too little—but I am learning that He desires my company anyway.

A couple of summers ago I was asked to perform in Ohio. A converted barn had become the concert venue for a very successful folk music series. It was rumored to be a rare haven for singer/songwriters, and I was excited and nervous in equal parts. My duo partner Spencer was to meet me at the Canton airport—his work on violin, mandolin, and guitar was my secret weapon. We looked forward to the show for a very long time.

Spencer never arrived. An unpleasant encounter with some United States Customs and Immigration officers forced him to miss his flight. I was already unpacking at the farmhouse next to the barn/concert hall when I got his call. His voice was thick with disappointment, and even as I made a halfhearted attempt to console him, panic was setting in. How was I going to go on alone? "I'm so sorry," Spencer said. "I can't believe I'm missing it. And who's going to pray with you before the show?"

This was an odd thing for Spencer to say. We had discovered early on that praying together before our performances was as critical as tuning our instruments, but we never discussed it much. We just did it. Spencer's faith is deep and abiding, but he hates pious talk and religiosity with a particular passion. Besides, I could pray by myself. Still, his comment revealed a concern for me that gave me what my friend Bernie calls an AWFATH (an Actual Warm Feeling Around The Heart)—and I was glad he was my friend.

I hung up the phone and started tuning the guitars by myself. I was miserable, overwhelmed at having to engage a sold-out audience for two hours with no support. I tried to pray but I couldn't focus. The opening act began to play and set a clock ticking ominously in my head. Twenty minutes till show time. Feeling claustrophobic, I headed for the front porch. If I was going to hyperventilate, I may as well do it in the fresh country air.

I had only been fighting off the mosquitoes a few minutes when a woman got up from a folding chair at the back of the barn and starting walking hesitantly toward me. I stiffened. I didn't want to sign any autographs while the first singer was performing. I would hate to become a distraction from his show, and I needed to be alone and collect my thoughts. But the lady kept coming. I worked up the most sincere smile I could manage while scanning the area for security personnel. "Excuse me," she said, barely above a whisper, "I am so sorry to bother you. I feel foolish. But sitting over there watching the show, I got the strangest sense I was supposed to come pray with you." I swallowed hard and managed an eloquent response along the lines of "Oh." She prayed a short and sweet and inspired prayer—asking God to be with me through my performance—and then she left.

As she headed back to the barn she stepped out of the way of another woman who was moving unmistakably in my direction. "Excuse me," whispered the new stranger, "I hope you won't think this is weird, but I just felt I should come pray with you. Is that OK?" I told her that it was.

By the time I took the stage, four women I had never met before had prayed with me. And God had spoken. *Come on, talk to Me. This is important. And if you can do it in the company of your brothers and sisters, even better.*

———————

Of course, there are a few other things I'd like to ask God about prayer. Can our requests change the course of history? Can we actually change God's mind and will? Are the hand of fate and the hand of God locked in some sort of arm wrestle that hinges on our petitions? I have received certain and dramatic answers to some of my prayers. I have been able to perceive nothing but the deafening roar of silence to others. In some cases I have eventually discovered why my prayers were answered with a "no" or a "not yet." In many others I remain bewildered. But I am hopeful that more will be revealed—and I suspect that at least some of my frustration has more to do with my ability to listen than with God's willingness to speak. Regardless, I will pray, because He has asked me to, because understanding follows obedience, and because my life would not be worth living if I could not cry out to the God who gave it to me.

However uncertain I am about the way prayer changes the unfolding of events, I have been shown clearly that prayer changes *me*. When I begin to pray for an enemy, my heart like a fist clenched with anger, I am opened up until I can no longer hold the resentment and frustration. When I plead with the publican, "Lord, have mercy on me, a sinner," I travel a little deeper into the mercy of God. When I confess with the father who cried out, "I believe, help my unbelief," my faith is made a little stronger.

Sometimes, when I offer up a prayer of intercession for someone else, I discover that in some mysterious way God actually uses my prayer as a channel for His grace. My whispered petition brings down such an outpouring of His love that I can't help but wonder if He's just been waiting for an opening.

And so I pray. Whether I am on a front porch in Saskatchewan or Ohio, whether I am praying from a surrendered or a stubborn heart, I speak with the God of Creation. I am ushered—sometimes reverent, sometimes willful, never worthy—into His presence, and when the language is beyond me it is spoken on my behalf. I pray for the wisdom to learn more about prayer, and for the courage to pray the prayers that will change me. And in my best and bravest moments, when I ache to know more of the tremendous and fascinating mystery of God, I pray for rain.

Then you will call upon me and come and pray to me, and I will listen to you. You will seek me and find me when you seek me with all your heart.

Jeremiah 29:12-13

We talk about heaven being so far away. It is within speaking distance to those who belong there.

Dwight L. Moody

9

Forget-Me-Nots

I have a packet of flower seeds I keep close at hand. I keep telling myself I'm going to grow them—perhaps one of these springs I will undergo a radical personality change and turn into a gardener worthy of my Bittner roots. Until then, this little packet will stay firmly planted in the pocket of my black winter coat. I rub the envelope of seeds between my decidedly un-green thumb and my forefinger, like a good luck charm, and sometimes I pull it out and absently reread the inscription on the package: "FOR-GET-ME-NOTS. Support your local Alzheimer's Society."

There is Alzheimer's on both sides of our family. Mark and I joke about it, cavalierly referring to occasional memory lapses as "Sometimers"—as if making light of the skeletons in our genetic closets could lessen our fear of them. Like millions of other people, we have learned to live with unspeakable sadness, resigning ourselves to the horror of watching this illness steal away someone we love. My mother-in-law, Jean, is in the throes of Alzheimer's now, and the disease has left few traces of the vibrant, creative, resourceful woman who raised seven children, including the rough-and-tumble boy who grew up to be the love of my life. In all of the conversations Mark and I have had regarding her care and the devastating effects of her illness, we have—by unspoken mutual consent—resolutely avoided discussing the very real possibility that the same thief lurks in the back alleys of our own DNA.

Although some of the most brilliant minds in the world have dedicated themselves to understanding Alzheimer's disease, it has belligerently remained an enigma. But just today I heard a newscast in the car—a radio announcer reading a heart-pounding, earthshaking report with professional indifference. Researchers in Florida have identified the cell receptor that makes traitors out of immune system cells and causes them to attack nerve cells in the brain of an Alzheimer's victim. The news is exciting because many medications have already been developed to block various cell receptors for the treatment of other diseases. It is possible that the right medication *already exists*. And so there is hope.

But even if scientists truly are beginning to demystify the disease, I have a few questions for the theologians. Alzheimer's, we are told, "gradually destroys the ability to reason, remember, imagine, and learn."[18] How can this be? Our intellect, our capacity to imagine, our memories—these are the cornerstones of who we are. I have always believed them to be the substance of our souls. It is one thing to live in a world where the physical body is subject to ruin, but how are we to reconcile the awareness that our very essence may be vulnerable to obliteration with the belief that God will never leave or forsake us? How do we partake in the story of redemption if we are at risk of having our own stories snatched from us? The reality that Alzheimer's (or anything else for that matter) has the authority to deconstruct us to such a devastating extent scares me to death. Is Alzheimer's a disease of the soul as well as the mind? I have looked into the vacant stare of an afflicted loved one, and I need to know—when Alzheimer's takes somebody away, where does he go?

My granddad had Alzheimer's disease. The year I turned 12 he grew weak and disoriented in a rapid decline, and before my fourteenth birthday I watched my grandmother lay flowers on his grave.

He was reticent even before he got sick, never really feeling the need to talk unless he had something in particular to say. He was so unassuming that I was repeatedly startled to discover the spark in his ice-blue eyes. I spent many meals at my grandparents' table, hot and bothered in my scratchy Sunday best, exasperated by the impossible challenge of keeping my elbows off the table. But before things could get too unbearable, my grandfather would wink at me and sneak me an icing-laden pastry, brazenly disregarding my uneaten vegetables. Laughter would twitch about his mouth, and I would giggle breathlessly with the thrill of our secret. One of my grandfather's quiet gifts was the ability to make anyone who was the object of his affection feel singularly special, and I believed I was the only one who could really make him smile.

The earliest memory I possess is a game of peekaboo at my grandparents' house. I am on my hands and knees creeping toward a doorway, and my granddad is waiting around the corner, ready to pounce and tickle and dance with me, cheek to bristly cheek. I remember endless games of blocks and trucks, and—as I grew older—billiards and darts in my grandparents' drafty basement. There were sleepy afternoons curled up together in his fuzzy brown easy chair, reading the Sunday comics. When I got too big for his lap we graduated to the back porch swing. I don't recall what we talked about. I mostly remember the snap of laundry waving at half-mast on the clothesline, and the hummingbirds humming at the feeder attached to the kitchen window.

I'm not certain how long he was ill before I began to notice changes in him. At first it was just that he spoke even less than normal and sometimes fumbled over my name. But the Alzheimer's progressed more aggressively than anyone anticipated, and his clear blue eyes grew cloudy until I could no longer detect their twinkle. I watched his son, my daddy, grow tense and troubled in his presence, and my young heart sustained its first adult-sized wound.

My grandparents lived in Victoria, on Vancouver

Island, and my brothers and I used to spend the weeks between our monthly visits filled with anxious anticipation. We relished the two-hour ferry ride from the mainland to Victoria, loved the boat's greasy cafeteria food and salty decks. When it rained we were allowed to play video games inside, and once we each got to buy one thing in the gift shop. I chose a pen that had a boat floating inside it—if you held the pen the right way you could make the boat travel from the Island to the Mainland. My grandparents were duly impressed.

We followed the same ritual every visit. The ship would dock at Schwartz Bay, and our parents would make us promise to walk the maze of corridors to the arrival terminal in an orderly fashion. It was a long walk, and the excitement would get the best of us until we were running and dodging the slower passengers to reach our destination. Our nana and granddad were always there, proffering chocolate bars and hugs and exclamations of how big we were getting.

Around the time I became too old and too cool to run with my brothers, we began to find my grandmother waiting for us alone at the terminal. "Granddad's in the car," she'd reassure us. "He's just a little too tired to make the walk." I would rush—as nonchalantly as possible—to the car. But he'd be sleeping, or staring out the window, and he never even said "hello."

I started to wish we didn't have to go to Victoria.

The last time I saw my granddad we were driving from my grandparents' house back to the ferry terminal. He was distant and sick, his breathing labored, and the rest of us rode together in a weary silence. I was wedged in the back seat between my granddad and my brother Chris, stiff and resentful and brokenhearted. If the grandfather I knew still existed, he had been locked away somewhere, hopelessly lost within the stranger beside me. The drive seemed to take forever.

Then my granddad cleared his throat as if he had something important to say. Collectively we held our breath, shocked and desperately hopeful. He hadn't uttered a word in weeks. He began to sing.

> *Blessed assurance, Jesus is mine*
> *O, what a foretaste of glory divine*

My dad was staring at the rearview mirror.

> *This is my story, this is my song*
> *Praising my Savior all the day long*[19]

There was a stunned silence. My grandfather cleared his throat again.

> *When we all get to heaven, what a day of rejoicing that will be*
> *When we all see Jesus, we'll sing and shout the victory*[20]

Someone in the front seat began to sing with him, and by the chorus we were all singing, even my restless little brothers. I permitted myself the luxury of relaxing my tense body enough to rest my head on my grandfather's shoulder. All the way to Schwartz Bay he kept singing—"How Great Thou Art," "When the Roll Is Called Up Yonder," "In the Sweet By and By"—leading his family in hymn after hymn until we reached the terminal and kissed him goodbye.

Six days later we were back at Schwartz Bay, hot and bothered in our scratchy Sunday best, and my grandmother was waiting at the terminal alone. We all embraced in a tear-stained huddle. And then we went to my grandfather's funeral. I cried so hard I thought I might throw up. But when the organ wheezed into life I sang with all my might, believing with every inch of my heart that the God of my father's father had personally arranged that bon voyage party in my grandparents' Oldsmobile.

> *In the sweet by and by*
> *We shall meet on that beautiful shore*
> *In the sweet by and by*
> *We shall meet on that beautiful shore*[21]

Telling the story now I am almost embarrassed by it—it feels suspiciously like I've dreamed up some impossibly sweet Movie of the Week ending to an otherwise tragic plot. But it really happened. Sometimes life is as unbelievably beautiful as it is cruel.

Through my mother-in-law's illness I have learned a lot more about Alzheimer's than I could have understood in my early teens. I have discovered, for example, that it is not uncommon for Alzheimer's patients to remember the hymns of their youth. This in no way lessens my conviction that what happened in the car that day was a miracle—unlike many others stricken with the disease, my grandfather had not sung at all during his illness before that occasion. But I also consider it a miracle that some people with Alzheimer's habitually sing the songs they loved growing up. This seems to me to be a sign that some transcendent, defining element of personality is outlasting the disease. Watching the patients on Jean's ward, it has occurred to me once or twice that rather than robbing an individual's core identity, the disease may actually be stripping away everything but the essence of that person.

My mom claims her 30 years of nursing have taught her that illness has a way of revealing the real character of the person afflicted. The truly lovely become lovelier, and the genuinely nasty become nastier. Alzheimer's, on the other hand, can be deceiving—sometimes causing aggression even among very gentle men and women. Still, I can sit in the common areas of Jean's care home and learn a lot about the people who live there. I can see the Class Clown still lurking behind the slightly crazy grin of the man in the red plaid pajamas, the Mother Hen gossiping away (now to no one in particular) in the corner, the Teacher lecturing—with just a hint of condescension—to the Listener in the wheelchair next to him. And when Jean walks in the room, I see the Nurturer, the Mother. I see love.

This woman—who at one point had a ten-year-old, a six-year-old, five children under the age of five, and no electric washer or dryer—is my hero. She may even be superhuman—her twin boys weighed over 9 lbs. and 8 lbs. respectively, combining for close to a whopping 18 lbs. of baby and securing her the record for twin birth weights at St. Joseph's Hospital in London, Ontario. Raising seven children with little money required a plan. Jean had one. Hockey in the living room was permitted, breaking of windows was not. Desserts were cut into eight pieces, and the coveted eighth piece was given to whichever child most liked that particular confection (meaning she had to develop at least seven regular desserts so everybody could have a favorite). Wardrobes were color-coded. (I never understood why Mark always wore brown until I learned some relevant family history— he was the third boy, so blue and green were already taken.) And when the blues and greens and browns got dirty, my mother-in-law scrubbed them in her wringer washer, usually humming her favorite big band tunes.

In 1991, Jean lost her youngest and most fragile daughter to pneumonia, and grief gave her Alzheimer's disease the ammunition it needed to launch an aggressive and relentless attack. Today she no longer recognizes her loved ones by name— in fact, she so frequently drifts back to younger days that she often mistakes Mark for her brother. But when her children come to visit she responds to them with an infinite tenderness, touching their faces and murmuring genuinely delighted *hellos* and *how are yous?*

They miss her terribly, of course, even when they are in the same room with her. They wonder where she spends her time, and whether she remembers them in their school days or is lost back in her own. I have never left her ward without tears obscuring my vision. One of the only three times I have ever seen my husband cry was at her side, feeding her strained vegetables, his tears spilling onto her plate while she stroked his face with utter love.

How did we get here? How did we fall far enough to

land in a world where the reward for a life spent giving is the loss of the capacity to reason, remember, imagine, or learn? It is grotesquely unfair. But what about the original question? Does the loss of the intellect and memory—the theft of our stories—mean the loss of the soul? Watching my husband's mother take his hand and walk quietly with him down the halls of her care home, I will not deny that housed somewhere within her weakened body there is *something* (I cannot give it a word any more precise than that) that transcends reason and memory and the DNA that scripted both her wonderful tenderness and her treacherous Alzheimer's. It is a tragedy when Alzheimer's steals the keys of reason, memory, and imagination—leaving its victim maddeningly dead-bolted away from the people she loves with no way of turning the lock. But maybe the soul is something *other* than what we can identify and define and sometimes even reach— maybe our cognitive powers are points of access to the soul rather than the soul itself.

I have always believed that the last time I saw my grandfather was a gift from God—a chance to say "farewell" and to rest assured that I would see him again in heaven. But I have begun to suspect lately that those holy moments were also a sign—a promise that wherever my granddad was in the last difficult months of his life, God was there too. And if that is true, then I know also that God has not left or forsaken Jean, and that—wherever I am now or may someday be—He will not forsake me either. This is the story my grandfather told me—even when he was stripped of memory and cognition—and I realize just now, as I type this sentence, the significance of his last words to me:

This is my story, this is my song
Praising my Savior all the day long

You could tell me that God is God, whether we acknowledge Him or not, and that He is present, whether we feel Him or not, and I would not disagree. But I will go one essential step further and tell you that I cannot believe that my grandfather—even at his most debilitated—was merely an unaware object of God's love. In some dimension he remained in communication with the Lover of his soul, and I suspect that the grace extended in allowing him to come back to the surface long enough to say goodbye was not anything he needed, but rather a gift to those of us who remained on this shore.

You could tell me that nothing can take away the legacy of my grandfather and my husband's mother, that their blood runs through the veins of their children and their children's children, and that nothing can erase the lives they lived or the impact they had on all who crossed their paths. I would agree that indeed they have achieved that sort of immortality. But there is more to it than that, and the one thing I am most certain of is that in and of themselves they are eternal. I see now what grief obscured when my grandfather was slipping away—that even at his most unrecognizable there were foretastes of glory and intimations of immortality in every fiber of his being.

We are fragile and vulnerable, our lives are fleeting vapors. This is a hard truth, and no amount of philosophizing or fervent belief can make it easy. And yet it seems there is some part of ourselves—deeper than language, higher than cognition, more defining than even our memories—that the very worst of life cannot take away. Even stripped of the stories that comprise our lives, our lives tell a story, and a life surrendered to God will tell *the* story of His love long after words have failed. At my most faithful—perhaps when I most resemble my grandfather—I am convinced that neither death nor life, neither angels nor demons, neither the present nor the future, nor any powers, neither height nor depth, nor anything else in all of creation can separate us from the love of God.[22] And so I am also convinced that nothing, not Alzheimer's nor any other physical or emotional trauma, can divorce us with any finality from whatever there is within us that bears His image. Like flowers breaking through sidewalk cement, our souls endure under the greatest adversity—Forget-Me-Nots stubbornly blooming even in the cracks of our brokenness.

Where can I go from your Spirit? Where can I flee from your presence? If I go up to the heavens, you are there; if I make my bed in the depths, you are there. If I rise on the wings of the dawn, if I settle on the far side of the sea, even there your hand will guide me, your right hand will hold me fast. If I say "Surely the darkness will hide me and the light become night around me," even the darkness will not be dark to you; the night will shine like the day, for darkness is as light to you.

Psalm 139:7-12

10

A Little Brother

I was the one who answered the phone when my grandmother called to say that my grandfather had passed away. I remember that her voice sounded strange, strangled almost. She didn't even say "hello" to me, or ask how I was feeling, which seemed odd, because she knew I had pneumonia. She asked for my father, and I yelled for him to pick up the extension downstairs. I kept listening—not to eavesdrop, just to make sure he came on the line—but I stayed on a moment too long and I heard her say, "Dad's gone. He's gone." Then I hung up the phone and sat in my favorite place—the couple of cozy feet of carpet between the wall and the edge of my canopy bed (the same bed I had in kindergarten, the same bed I had until I was married), and I tried to breathe. A few years earlier, when we'd been playing street hockey (like good Canadian kids) on the cul-de-sac in front of our house, Chris had accidentally shot a tennis ball directly into my stomach. The wind had gone clear out of me, leaving me gasping for air in a disoriented panic, shocked that my body could betray me like that—could just stop drawing in oxygen when there was plenty around for the taking. I'd forgotten what that felt like until I heard my nana's voice. Now I was winded again—shocked and betrayed. Of course, the pneumonia wasn't helping my breathing either.

All things considered, it was the worst of times for the Jonat family. The terrible economic crash of the early 1980s had hit close to home, and the real estate investments everyone had deemed foolproof ended up proving everyone fools. My parents survived—just barely—but they sustained some considerable financial wounds. Two years earlier, out of a desire to move closer to our church, they had found a lot on Dansey Avenue (not far from Blue Mountain Street) and decided to build the dream house they'd been imagining for years. They had poured themselves into every facet of its creation, from designing the floor plan to planting the hedges. Now they were forced to sell it, and even after they had unceremoniously handed the keys to the strangers who would inhabit their dream, the financial strain was still serious.

My mom had no choice but to return to the work-force, securing a nursing job for the first time in seven years. The medical world had changed considerably, and she felt rusty and disoriented in the hospital. Having cherished her role as a stay-at-home mother, she hated leaving her kids during her nursing shifts. And though I didn't comprehend it at the time, I can see now that she was hauling around a heavy load on her tired, narrow shoulders. She could not understand what in the world God was doing.

Meanwhile, the good folks of Blue Mountain Baptist—the congregation we had moved to be near—were going through a very bad time. There was a group within the church who questioned the leadership of the pastor, and people began conducting themselves in shameful ways that surprised even themselves. Women who had taught me my Sunday school lessons were heard screaming at each other in the hallways of the church. There were accusations and tears and—eventually—cold, hard silences where there used to be warm familiarity. It was my first exposure to Ugliness in the Name of Religion, and it was devastating. My father— Chairman of the Deacon's Board— was caught in the middle, trying desperately and vainly to mediate. The church split right in two, and so, it seemed to me, did my dad. My mom got sadder.

That was when we all caught pneumonia, and then somewhere in the middle of the pneumonia, my granddad died. I remember Mr. Hayes, a friend from church (one of the ones who was still friendly), stopping by for a visit, right after we got back from the funeral in Victoria. "Just wanted to see how Job and his family were doing tonight," he said. After he left, I curled up in my favorite spot between the bed and the wall and read the book of Job for the very first time, searching for clues. I found it hard to understand.

The most pressing and immediate problem was that my mom was too newly employed to be able to take any time off, and while the rest of us were recovering from our illness, my six-year-old brother, Cameron, was getting sicker. So I stayed home from school to take care of him. Everyone thought I was very noble for doing this, but even though I was terribly worried about Cam (especially the couple of days when his fever spiked dangerously high), I loved caring for him. After months of feeling utterly helpless in the midst of my family's troubles, I was finally needed. I could help make things better. And best of all, I got to dote on my little brother, who—truth be told—has always had a smile like sunshine and complete possession of my heart. I kept cool washcloths on his forehead, nagged him to drink his orange juice, and made sure the TV was on for *Sesame Street*. When he was extra sleepy and miserable, I called him "Mommy's Little Soldier" on behalf of our mother, because he had confessed to me in a moment of feverish weakness that it was his favorite nickname.

Eventually Cam's fever broke, and before long he was once again a boisterous, brawny boy who would throw a pillow at my head if I ever dared to call him "Mommy's Little Soldier" again. Things began to get better. My mom got used to the new hospital and remembered she was an excellent nurse. We all discovered we really didn't mind our new house on Dennison Avenue, which was actually even closer to the church, and after a while we didn't miss Dansey Avenue quite so much. Blue Mountain Baptist began to haltingly put itself back together. We endured.

Those events took place almost two decades ago, and they seldom come up in family conversation. But for some reason—maybe because I have been writing and thinking about the seasons when life is messy and mysterious—my mother and I ended up talking about that time over the phone the other night. We both know other families who have faced much greater tragedies, and yet neither my mom nor I can deny the lasting effects of our own difficult season. She told me that back then her grief and confusion and—most of all—her unanswered questions had rumbled beneath her feet like little earthquakes, leaving the concrete foundation of her faith shot through with hairline fractures. The cracks, she admitted, had never really gone away, not completely. If anyone on this tilting planet is a believer, it is my mother. But she is also honest. And she still doesn't understand, eighteen years later, what in the world God was doing. She loves Him anyway. But she wishes she could make better sense of Him, or at least of the life lived under His gaze.

While we were talking, my mother made a quick laundry list of the problems we had faced. "Granddad died." (This was the worst of it, of course.) "We lost the house. The church split. You kids got sick, and it just about killed me to have to leave you at home while I went to work." With a heavy sigh, she began to fill in some of the details I had not previously known. "Here is what made it so hard," she confessed. "I told the hospital I would only take night shifts so that I could be home during the day for you and your brothers. But they said I had to start with an orientation period of two weeks of day shifts. I prayed—over and over and over again—that for just those two weeks, no one in the family would get sick. And then you all got pneumonia—even Granddad. I couldn't believe it. You missed all that school taking care of Cam, which was so unfair to you, and—"

"Mom," I interrupted, without thinking, "the part about me taking care of Cam, honestly, that is probably one of the nicest memories of my life. I don't think he and I would be as close as we are now if it hadn't happened."

There was nothing but silence on the other end of the phone line. I became worried, thinking maybe I'd been too chipper about a horrible time in my mother's history. "Don't get me wrong," I said lamely. "We really needed you. It was just good to spend so much time with Cam when he was that young."

There was another long pause. And then my mother, her voice quaking with emotion, said, "You intended it for harm, but God intended it for good." At first I was confused, and began to protest that I certainly had never meant her any harm. Then I realized she was paraphrasing Joseph—the great scene in Genesis when Joseph reassures his brothers that God has used their dastardly deed (throwing him into a pit because he got on their nerves) to bring about great good (exalting Joseph to a place of leadership in Egypt, and using him to save thousands of lives in a time of famine).

"Oh," I said to my mom. "I see." And I did. For eighteen years my mother remembered the time I'd had to spend taking care of Cam with regret—wondering why we'd been burdened with yet another difficulty in the midst of our family's trials—and now I was telling her matter-of-factly that it had been an industrial-sized, bona fide blessing.

In our case, of course, no particular villain threw us into the pit. I don't think anyone in my family can identify for sure the source of our troubles. Satan? Maybe. The consequences of our own mistakes? Probably, at least with respect to our financial woes. But we are mostly inclined to see our trials as the random, natural, and ultimately unavoidable pitfalls of living in a fallen world. We recognize not only the forces of evil, but the forces of gravity. To put it as succinctly and as unprofanely as possible: stuff happens. Really bad stuff sometimes. But even the troubles that seem hell-bent on bringing us harm God can intend for good. He can take some detail from the worst of times and redeem it into something better than we could have imagined. Every once in a while (usually when we least expect it), He turns catastrophe into what Tolkein coined eucatastrophe, turning tragedy into happy ending—like the best fairy tales, only better.

Unfortunately, there is no formula—God is not remotely predictable in terms of when and how He brings about these mysterious and wonderful transformations. The happy endings are the exception, not the rule. If He intended to reconfigure the circumstances of my parents' financial loss or the fracturing of our church for some particular good, I have yet to discern it. Maybe the redemption in these cases is more subtle—developments in our faith and character that would never have occurred in the absence of our trials. The story is certainly not over—perhaps more will be revealed. Perhaps not. Either way, it seems to me that in those rare instances when a catastrophe *does* turn suddenly and inexplicably into an impossibly wonderful eucatastrophe, God—who is always present in our lives, but seldom recognized—is clearing His throat, dropping a hint, leaving a divine calling card for us to trace back to Him. I suspect that we all get the odd Joseph-in-Egypt moment (or, in my case, bonding-with-little-brother moment) as a promise that God is also working in all the other murkier moments, the times when He is less easily detected. That is why, when harm is headed my way and good is nowhere in sight, I sometimes call my brother Cam, just to hear his voice.

God has actually used my brown-eyed little brother for the purposes of demonstration more than once. I can still clearly remember the day in 1976 when, after loading way too many bags of groceries into the trunk of our Chevrolet, my mother climbed behind the wheel, started the car, stopped it again, and swiveled around to face Chris and me in the backseat. "What would you like more than anything else in the world?" she asked, obviously excited about something. Chris and I consulted. "A puppy?" he asked hopefully. Our mother shook her head. I tried the next logical option. "A horse?" Still no. "Fish?" we ventured. My mother couldn't stand it any longer. "A little brother!" she hollered. "Or a sister! And you'll get one this week!"

We were confused. At eight and six, we were not entirely clear on how babies were made, but we were fairly certain that once a baby got started, its mommy's tummy grew big. We quickly scanned our mother. She looked like she always did. Something wasn't adding up. She rolled down the windows, settling in for a talk, and she began to explain what the word "adoption" meant. Once we were somewhat clear on that concept, she added an even headier idea. "You know how hard it was for us to move here when Daddy got transferred?" (We were living in the foreign land of Quebec, and we missed the West Coast terribly.) "Well, it turns out there was a very good reason for us to be here. Your little brother or sister was waiting for us, and we didn't even know it!"

The last part was not entirely true—we found out years later that somehow my mother *had* known a child was waiting for her in Quebec. Even as high school sweethearts my parents had envisioned having two children and adopting a third. Chris and I were oblivious to the fact that just a few days before my father had gotten word of his transfer, a Vancouver-based adoption had fallen through. The day my dad called my mom from work to tell her—with a certain amount of dread—that they would have to leave everything familiar to move 3000 miles across Canada, she had startled him with her matter-of-fact response. "Oh. I guess that's because our baby will be waiting for us there." After that, the more her concerned friends and relatives had tried to caution her against letting her hopes rise too high (after all, the odds were against an adoption working out), the more my mother had insisted that this was a little secret God had let her in on. He had something—someone—in mind, she was sure of it. Later, even when Cam's birth mother started to doubt that she would be able to go ahead with the adoption, my mother—contrary to her anxious temperament—never doubted that all would be well. She did, however, restrain herself from informing Chris and me of her conviction until that day in the Chevrolet, when at last her child's impending arrival had been confirmed, and she simply couldn't keep it to herself another second.

Just as our mother predicted, Cameron came bellowing into the world within a week. Four days later, he came home, wrapped in a blue flannel blanket. The adoption had been arranged through an agency connected with our church, so the pastor was the one who brought him to us. Some other people came, too—deacons, maybe, or other officials associated with the agency—but I don't remember much about them. They were the spectators. Me, Chris, my mom and dad, and the baby in the blue flannel blanket—we were the participants. I was a child, but I knew a miracle when I saw one. His name was Cam, and he was ours.

There was a lot of activity—people scurrying in and out of the kitchen with steamy mugs and sandwiches, cameras flashing, Chris and I fidgeting nervously on the couch, waiting for our turn to hold the baby. The pastor prayed a prayer of dedication; someone else made a little speech. My father hovered, leaving now and then to put on another pot of coffee but always returning to my mother's side. She, it seemed, was in an entirely different world. (In my memory she is moving in slow motion while everyone else scurries around the periphery at hyper-speed.) She sat in the center of the living room—the eye of the hurricane—completely oblivious to the surrounding commotion, utterly at peace, holding her child. She sang and she cooed and she rocked and she cried.

My mother's tears were clearly expressions of joy, but I know now there was a sadness mingled in them too— an awareness that somewhere across town another mother sat with empty arms and a heart crushed beneath the weight of her sacrifice. The woman who bore my little brother must have believed at first that her pregnancy could bring only harm. She was single, shamed by her mistake, strapped for resources, trapped. But as the baby grew within her so did hope, and courage, and I believe she must have seen a vision of God turning harm into good. *Cam.* She gave him life, and when he was four days old, she gave him to us. Ever since we met him we have loved him as our own—except that, clearly, he is God's.

The day our family of four became a family of five I began to glimpse a truth that I never could have articulated then—I struggle to put it into words now. At eight, I had only the vaguest sense of the pain Cameron's birth mother endured to give us the joy of loving him, but it was enough to plant within me the seed of an idea. *The most precious things are also the most costly.* Watching my mother weep over my new brother, a certain foundation was laid within my soul, so that—for the rest of my life—every struggle could increasingly confirm in me the suspicion that everything worth anything comes at a price. This understanding has helped me to find grounds for hope in even the worst of times—the recognition that if things are difficult, I've likely stumbled onto the start of something important.

But the lessons I learned back in 1976 also serve an even greater, more sacred purpose. With the gift of my brother came an awareness that whenever a great good is brought out of the evil in this world, somewhere a sacrifice has been made. An appreciation of that particular mystery has been for me the beginning of an encounter with an even holier one—the first shreds of any real understanding of salvation. When I survey the cross, I am able to glimpse at least a little of the ultimate sacrifice made on my behalf. When I am told that a price had to be paid so that I could become a child of God, the concept does not seem as strange or foreign as it otherwise might, and I am able to recognize it as truth.

Last March Cam turned 23, and a month later, he was married. He and his bride looked fabulous, but of course I barely saw them. I was looking instead at a four-day-old miracle, wrapped in a blue flannel blanket, and at a six-year-old little soldier dependent on his sister for Kleenex and comfort. I was remembering all the great things Cameron Jonat has been and will undoubtedly be. Crying there in my pew, I found myself praying...and for once I was not grilling God about the source of our trials or the ways He does and does not intervene. "God," I whispered, as my brother kissed his new wife, "You are very, very good."

March 23, 1997

Dear Cam,

I don't know if I've ever written you a letter before. I do know that I've never tried to properly tell you what you have added to my life. On the occasion of your twenty-first birthday (give or take a few days) I feel suddenly compelled to attempt both. I hope you will indulge me.

I will never, for as long as I live, forget the day they brought your still pointy-headed, adorable little self to our house in Beaconsfield. The first time I held you, I felt a kind of awe and wonder I'd never felt before (and have seldom felt since)—a mysterious certainty that you were nothing less than an extraordinary gift direct from God. I loved you with an intensity that was almost more than an eight-year-old big sister could take.

Funny thing is, I still feel that way about you. Last night, watching you drum at D'arby's, the gratitude I feel just for the chance to know you washed over me again. Cam, I am so proud of who you have become. You are funny and charismatic, brave and free-spirited, strong and compassionate. I love you with an intensity that is almost more than a twenty-nine-year-old big sister can take.

The sight of you has been making me smile for twenty-one years now. Thank you.

Before I finish mushing like this (who knows when I'll be so inclined again?), I want you to know how happy I am that you are getting a chance to know some of your biological family. Don't ever feel that to love them is to betray

Mom, Dad, Chris, or me in any imaginable way. One of the things that your arrival on the scene taught me is that the more people you let into your heart, the bigger your heart gets. The more love you give, the more love you have to give. It just keeps growing.

Little Brother, you have a very big heart. I'm looking forward to watching it continue to grow for the next fifty or sixty years.

Happy Birthday.

Love,
Carolyn

11

The
Telephone
Pole

Our home on Dennison Avenue was barely a stone's throw away from Blue Mountain Park, and the park was only another few blocks away from Como Lake Junior Secondary School—the site of my eighth-, ninth-, and tenth-grade adventures. The walk home from school took a maximum of 15 minutes, but it was often more trouble than one would expect. Every afternoon, bent beneath the weight of an overstuffed book bag and an alto saxophone, I would clump down the front steps of the school and begin to meander my way past the school building, the football field, and the running track. By the time I was weaving along the uneven stretch of sidewalk that bordered the park—trees to my right, a narrow field of gravel and parked cars to my left—I was invariably lost in another world.

Sometimes it would be the writing of a song that distracted me—by the time I had crossed Blue Mountain Street and reached Dennison Avenue I would have a few carefully rhymed lines completed and no idea how I had gotten home. Other days, I would disappear into the plot of whatever book I was currently reading. While my feet dutifully carried me in the right general direction, my mind would be entirely elsewhere, living out the plight of the novel's heroine, trying desperately to see into her future.

Anytime there had been a relational trauma at school—my friend Allison breaking up with my friend Brad, for example, or Brad's friend Michael breaking up with his girlfriend Dana because he suspected she liked Scott, who secretly liked Allison—I would spend the trek home preoccupied with the problem, hypothesizing its solution, and imagining the helpful dialogue I would have with the parties involved during the next day's lunch. But sometimes I would devote myself to crises even bigger than the ones Brad and Allison were facing. The days my social studies teacher had been particularly inspiring, my journey towards Blue Mountain Street would be consumed with analyzing the world hunger problem, achieving peace in the Middle East, or solving any other equally worrisome global dilemma. While nothing much usually happened during the short walk home, in my head it was always eventful.

About two-thirds of the way across the park, there was a telephone pole that—for some inexplicably sinister reason—had been hazardously planted right in the middle of the sidewalk. Traveling on autopilot, I would forget to watch for the pole. And so, on numerous occasions (I stopped keeping track of the exact number, but it was definitely more than five and—one can only hope—less than ten), that rough, wooden, malevolent post would appear out of nowhere, and I would walk smack into it. Hard. I would be knocked out of my reverie and on to my posterior, and it would hurt. Usually an elbow or knee would be wounded almost as badly as my pride. I would look around furtively to see if anyone had witnessed the collision, and then I would gather up my books, my saxophone, my glasses, and myself, do my best to brush off any debris, and hobble the rest of the way home.

Unfortunately, I was not particularly good at learning from these jarring experiences. Typically, by the time I reached the crosswalk at Blue Mountain Street, I would be preoccupied once again—no doubt lost in thought contemplating my tendency to get lost in thought—and more than once I stepped out into the busy traffic without even realizing I'd left the sidewalk. It's a wonder I survived.

I'm still alive, so evidently I've learned over the years to pay more attention to my surroundings. I've gotten better at negotiating the physical world, fraught as it is with telephone poles and oncoming traffic. Still, my natural inclination is to notice the minutiae of my interior landscape much more readily than the features of my exterior environment. After a visit to a friend's house, for example, I can tell you in precise detail the emotional, psychological, and spiritual implications of our conversation without ever having noticed she's lost 30 pounds or redone the wallpaper. Last year, while I was away from home on tour, my husband proudly reported to me over the phone that he had completed extensive repairs to our backyard fence, to which I replied—without thinking, and much to his consternation—"We have a fence?"

In my defense I will suggest there is an upside to my particular temperament. My tendency to lose myself in another universe has served me well in at least one respect. It has trained my soul to instinctively recognize a mystery that is foundational to faith—the secret that there is a realm beyond this physical world.

Years ago, Pastor Les Goertz (a gregarious, open-hearted man who used to shepherd the Blue Mountain flock) taught me that most people don't jump from a state of pagan indifference to a sudden acceptance of the gospel. Instead, they go through various stages of understanding that lead them, step-by-step, on a journey toward God. Before someone can accept the forgiveness of his sins, for example, he needs to discover first that there is, in fact, such a thing as evil—not only in the world, but in his heart. Before he can embrace God as the only reality that can fill the void inside him, he must first encounter the hard truth that nothing on this planet can be trusted to never let him down; no human can permanently satisfy the yearning of his soul. In our material, form-over-content world, it takes many of us a good while to recognize we even have a soul, let alone to figure out that it needs satisfying or saving.

When we begin to truly encounter God, our journey consists of grappling with these and other mysteries. We struggle to see beyond the human obsession with clocks and calendars—with temporal, chronological time (*chronos*)—in order to embrace the enigmatic promise of an eternal existence (*kairos*). We must transcend our fixation with atoms and subatoms—the reality we can see and quantify—in order to acknowledge there is another domain which remains unseen and immeasurable. Here is where I have an edge. While many of the other mysteries of life leave me baffled, thanks to my run-ins with the telephone pole it has never been hard for me to understand that we walk in two worlds—that there is another kind of time and a different kind of space, a dimension beyond our material existence. I have the bruises to prove it. And once, on an August night when I was 11, I moved spontaneously and instinctually into *kairos*, and somehow recognized it for what it was.

For several years in a row, we traveled with our family friends, the Daweses, to Penticton, a town in the orchard-graced interior of British Columbia that managed to feel small and sleepy even when it swelled with summer tourists. It was always fun to vacation with the Daweses, who were quite famous for their six striking, "L"-named daughters. I was fond of dazzling waitresses and lifeguards with a swift, dramatic recitation of the Dawes girls' names: *Leanne, Laurisa, Lynette, Loralee, Loreal, and Lana...thank you very much!* We all slept in a motel across the street from the lake, but we spent every waking moment at the beach, searching out Ogopogo (Penticton's innocuous version of the Loch Ness Monster), making sand castles, floating on air mattresses, and swimming until our parents made us stop.

One night, after the youngest kids had already snuggled down between the scratchy motel sheets, Chris and I went with the older girls back to the lake. We spent some time chasing each other around the beach—a jumble of sandy limbs and sun-bleached hair—still young enough to be completely unselfconscious in our swimsuits and totally abandoned to our fun. After a while, the other kids got hungry and began to wander back across the street, but I couldn't bring myself to leave. I walked out into the lake and stood there alone, the water lapping around my waist.

The lake was warmer than the dusky air, so I was half-chilled, half-warmed, and entirely covered in goose bumps. In the stillness of the now-deserted beach it seemed the breeze must be dancing across the surface of the lake just for me, and gratitude flowed through my body—sort of like hot chocolate does when you drink it down on a cold night and feel it streaming slowly toward your toes. I was very awake and aware, and peaceful at the same time, and even then I somehow sensed that to experience those states simultaneously was a rare gift indeed.

The sun set late on August nights, and as it began to sink into the dusk it reached out with dark golden rays to fingerpaint the sky with streaks of pink and orange. I remember thinking that if a painter attempted to brush his canvas with equally intense colors, he'd never sell his painting. It would seem too fake, too impossibly beautiful. I named the scene before me "Rapture Sky," explaining to myself that when Jesus finally broke through the clouds He would leave them soaked through with His radiance, and they would look just like they did now, except there would be trumpets too.

Standing there in the waters of Lake Okanagan, my soul rejoiced. That sounds more religious than it was—less real—but I can think of no more accurate way to put it. Though I had worshiped God on many occasions in the pews of Blue Mountain Baptist, I was aware for the first time that I was a part of something much greater than myself, my family, or my congregation. In some wordless way I cried *Holy!* and the moment I did I was ushered into another realm. I had not yet read much of the book of Revelation, and no one had told me there are creatures who surround the throne of God and never stop saying,

Holy, holy, holy
is the Lord God Almighty,
who was, and is, and is to come.[23]

But that night on that empty beach, I knew without a shadow of a doubt that I was not alone. All creation was worshiping with me, and so were the angels who bow down and tremble when someone dares to even whisper the name "Jesus." There was a great cloud of witnesses there too—all the saints who lived before me and live now in *kairos*. At eleven years old I could never have expressed this or defined it even for myself, but it was as palpable to me as the sand on my skin. Transfixed by beauty and transformed by something greater than beauty—the presence of God, hovering over the warm lake waters—I understood for the first time that when a soul truly worships, it becomes part of a cosmic song of praise that has always been and will always be. I was a witness in a great cloud of witnesses, and I was a citizen of an invisible kingdom—the City of God.

———————————

These days I am trying to pay better attention to my physical surroundings, not only for my personal safety and the safety of those around me, but also because this temporal realm is shot through with glory. The earth is alive with holy secrets—and there is very little here that God is not above using as a divine hint. Prairie storms and bright red canyons, leafs and lakes, strangers on the street—everything is sacred, because God chooses to give us glimpses of the supernatural here in the natural world. "The world is crowded with Him," C.S. Lewis says. "He walks everywhere *incognito*. And the *incognito* is not always hard to penetrate. The real labour is to remember, to attend. In fact, to come awake. Still more, to remain awake."[24]

Of course, the more I attend to the visible world, the more it ushers me into the invisible one, so I'm still having a little trouble keeping track of my surroundings. I've been writing this chapter mostly on planes, and in the course of one day of travel I have forgotten a sweatshirt at the LAX X-ray counter and a guitar at the baggage claim area in Vancouver. I suspect that I will continue to lose myself in another world for as long as I live in this one—and I am glad, because what I find there is worth immeasurably more than anything it costs me. But please...just warn me if you see an oncoming telephone pole.

So we fix our eyes not on what is seen, but on what is unseen. For what is seen is temporary, but what is unseen is eternal.

2 Corinthians 4:18

To see a world in a grain of sand
and heaven in a wild flower,
hold infinity in the palm of your hand
and eternity in an hour.

William Blake

12

St. Matthew's Passion

By the time I began my sophomore year at Trinity Western University, I was still carrying around overstuffed book bags and walking into things, but I had given up any serious study of the saxophone. I hated to waste all those years of lugging it home from school, but at the end of my freshman year I realized—in a sudden, luminous moment of clarity—that I was not a very good saxophonist. More to the point, I really did not want to haul the instrument around for one more day.

I did not, however, abandon my musical studies altogether. I was spending an inordinate amount of time in the rehearsal rooms, pounding out new songs on my guitar and the school's pianos, so it occurred to me that I should do something to legitimize my passion. I decided to add a minor in music to my studies in psychology and English. With my sax in mothballs, the jazz band was not an option, but there were plenty of other courses available. Unfortunately, one of the classes I selected was Music History 201. I was expecting an easy "A"—something along the lines of an innocuous introduction to "music appreciation." I was wrong.

On the first day of class, our professor—a brilliant and beleaguered organist named Mr. Rushton—cleared his throat, fumbled with his glasses, and began, "Right then. So we'll be getting acquainted with a few of the classics." He proceeded to hand out a 14-page list of the classics we would be expected to recognize. Our exams would consist of identifying—based on a thirty-second excerpt of music—the name of a particular work, which era over the last several hundred years it was from, who wrote it, why and how he wrote it, and what techniques he employed. My familiarity with these pieces was somewhat lacking. Once, in grade nine, my band teacher had given me a cassette of Mozart flute quartets, which I enjoyed very much and often played on Saturday mornings. Other than that, whenever anyone mentioned the classics, I tended to mostly think of the Rolling Stones and the Who. I was in big trouble.

Mr. Rushton made all the recordings of the works in question available in the library, but we couldn't sign them out—we had to listen to them *in* the library. This was a problem because I conducted most of my studies between the hours of midnight and 8 A.M., when the library was closed. Besides, the few times I did go to the library and set myself up with a turntable and a set of huge foam earphones, the magnificent classics of Western Civilization had the singular effect of putting me soundly to sleep. I would wake up at closing time—drooly, disoriented, and desperate.

My friend Sally was in the same class. She found it equally challenging, although she was a little more disciplined about the library listening sessions. Sometimes she would drag me out of my dorm at eight in the morning to run over to the library for a few frantic minutes of listening before our nine o'clock reckoning with Mr. Rushton. Neither of us would get a chance to shower, and we would arrive at the classroom wild-eyed, disheveled, and—on at least one notorious occasion—still wearing the previous night's acne cream on our faces. Mr. Rushton dubbed us "The Ugly Sisters." We became quite famous. But both of us were horrified by the realization that this one course was becoming a serious threat to our otherwise healthy grade point averages. We were failing.

I like to think that secretly Mr. Rushton was quite fond of us. Once, when we were stumbling away from the end of yet another grueling music history class, we ran into a blond-headed boy who explained he was looking for his daddy. Sal and I fell in love with the little guy long before we realized that his father was Mr. Rushton. In the middle of telling us his name, he suddenly froze in a Michelangelo-like pose and peered off into space with a marbly stare—which was his way of informing us that he really enjoyed playing "Statue." We thought it was a great game, and we got good at playing it too.

Mr. Rushton's son began to seek out the Ugly Sisters every time Mrs. Rushton dropped him off at the campus, and I suspect the time we spent playing with him gave our overworked professor a few extra minutes to tend to pressing matters—like grading our failing exams and preparing new, even more difficult ones. (Despite my fervent prayers, not once did Mr. Rushton test us on Mozart flute quartets.) He must have appreciated our spontaneous baby-sitting service because—just when it seemed our grades were sunk for sure—he threw us a life preserver. He gave us a chance to earn extra marks. All we had to do was attend, and prepare a report on, a performance of Bach's *St. Matthew's Passion*. We were pretty sure we could manage that.

The Vancouver Chamber Orchestra, the Vancouver Chamber Choir, and several renowned soloists were performing Bach's epic work at the Queen Elizabeth Theater. Sal and I bought tickets, along with four or five other desperate students. Of course, by the night of the performance, our gratitude had faded into resentment. We were all hopelessly behind on papers that were due for other classes, and final exams were looming ominously on the horizon. The last thing we had time for was a three-hour quasi-opera sung in German. It took us over an hour to drive into town and another 20 minutes to find parking. Once we had begrudgingly paid ten dollars to the parking attendant, we realized with dismay that we hadn't allowed enough time for dinner. Hunkering down in our theater seats, we were hungry and weary and radiating hostility.

I was confused for most of the first hour. Despite my German ancestry, I don't speak a word of the language, and even though I could ascertain the general plot—the suffering of Christ according to the book of Matthew—the finer points were lost on me. I spent a good deal of time concentrating on trying to open a bag of chocolate-covered peanuts (the only food on sale in the lobby) without making any noise. But once I had devoured my snack and calmed down a little, the music began to slip through the chinks in my armor. *St. Matthew's Passion*, I discovered, is a work to be reckoned with. Moving fluidly between moments of dark foreboding, strident tension, profound mourning, triumphant grandeur, and aching beauty, it demands response. My bad attitude was no match for Bach and his passion. Gradually, I was drawn into the drama unfolding on the stage.

By some mysterious process, I began to understand the scenes before me. The odd German word was close enough to English to provide a clue, but it was the music itself that somehow powerfully conveyed the tension and tragedy of the plot. One of the soloists was the "Evangelist"—his tenor voice provided haunting narration throughout the story. Another man with a darker baritone voice was Judas, and a third vocalist was Jesus. Each of the soloists would deliver the Gospel text in flowing recitations, and then the choir would respond—most often as the Faithful, but sometimes as the Angry Mob.

As the story unfolded a hard knot began to form in the pit of my stomach. The Last Supper. The Garden of Gethsemane. *Mein Vater,* Jesus sang, *ist's möglich, so gehe dieser Kelch von mir; doch nicht wie ich will, sondern wie du willst.* (My Father, if possible, allow this cup to pass from me; but not as I will, rather as thou wilt.) Then there was Judas' betrayal, the soldiers' capture of Jesus, and a long series of solos and choral responses—Jesus questioned, Jesus mocked, Jesus beaten.

A new soloist appeared—Pontius Pilate. The choir was transformed into an angry mob as Pilate asked whom he should spare—the thief Barabbas or Jesus.

Barrabam! the crowd cried in German, their polyphonic harmonies crashing together unbearably. *Barrabam! Barrabam!*

And then Pilate asked them:

> *Was soll ich denn machen mit Jesu, von dem gesagt wird, er sei Christus?*
> (What shall I then do with Jesus, of whom is said that He is Christ?)

And the mob replied:

> *ihn kreuzigen!*
> (Have Him crucified!)

The only word I really understood was the name, *Barrabam.* But that one word—cried zealously by the frenzied throng—said it all. Jesus stood before them—the Son of God reduced willingly to a fragile, broken man, all for the love of them—and without hesitation they chose whatever they could find instead of Him. *Give us that thief over there, Barabbas. Anything is better than Jesus. Crucify Him.*

I was completely undone. I hunched down as low as I could in my seat and buried my face in the crook of my arm, trying desperately to hide my sobs from my classmates and the rest of the audience. Bach's masterpiece had so stripped away my defenses that I was laid bare, and my heart was pierced with sorrow. The betrayal portrayed on the stage was unspeakable, inexplicable. And yet I suddenly knew it was no worse than the betrayal I was routinely capable of every time I chose any old thing I could find instead of Jesus.

Eight years earlier, I had learned in the waters of Lake Okanagan that I was—by my praise—part of the great cloud of witnesses who worship God. Now, I was learning in the plush red seats of the Queen Elizabeth Theater that I was—by my sin—part of the angry mob that crucifies Him. This new awareness was utterly devastating. And yet, at the same time, it plunged me deeply into a mystery too wonderful for words. *While we were still sinners, Christ died for us.*[25] I had heard and professed this glorious truth a hundred times. But I hadn't really begun to understand how unfathomable it truly is—while we are *hating* Him, demanding His death, choosing Barabbas, Christ dies for us. And even when we are something worse than the angry mob, when we are utterly, shatteringly indifferent to Him, Christ dies for us still. This is the deepest mystery of God—that He loves us. That He loves me.

By the time the performance was over, I could barely speak, and to this day Sal and I have never discussed that evening. I can't remember what I put in my report, but I passed the course. I told Mr. Rushton that I was grateful—I'm sure he thought I was thanking him for the extra marks. So I'll say it now. Thank you, Mr. Rushton, for giving me *St. Matthew's Passion.*

God answers. God speaks. And those who listen in the true humility of confession shall hear him clearly, for they will realize that the return of love is a divine gift. But those who do not confess will assume they deserve the love, and though God shall have said the same word to both, this latter group will hear no holy voice at all.

Walter Wangerin Jr.

Problem and Paradox

paradox: n. 1. a seemingly absurd or self-contradictory statement that is or may be true: religious truths are often expressed in paradox...
4. an opinion that conflicts with common belief

Collins English Dictionary

problem: n. Heaven will solve our problems, but not, I think, by showing us subtle reconciliations between all our apparently contradictory notions. The notions will all be knocked from under our feet. We shall see that there never was any problem.

C.S. Lewis

13

A Splendid Confusion

God, I can say with conviction, works in mysterious ways. Somehow a three-hour German opera became the key to the lock on my soul—opening me up to a truth I knew but did not really understand. I'd been singing "Jesus Loves Me" ever since I could form the words, but I hadn't even begun to perceive the enormity of what that meant until I got a brief, devastating glimpse of just how unworthy I was of Jesus' love. Christianity is rather emphatic about this particular paradox—we cannot understand how much we are valued until we perceive our own wretchedness. We cannot comprehend how beloved we are—the lengths God will go to in order to make us His children—until we see His sacrifice in the context of our unworthiness.

This is a challenging idea to process in a culture that—from the time we are born—earnestly exhorts us to believe in ourselves, to love ourselves, and to relentlessly seek the fulfillment of our own reportedly immense, inherent potential. The suggestion that we are thoroughly unworthy in our natural state flies in the face of everything we feel and think, and it really does not go over well at parties. But the thing is, I've tried believing in myself on enough occasions to know that such an endeavor is ill-advised. I can be counted on only to let myself down. And so it seems to me that a paradox that appears on the surface to confine and tear down the human spirit may turn out to be—oddly enough—the only thing that can set it free. I don't have to close my eyes, clench my fists, and—against all evidence to the contrary—believe in myself. I can believe in God instead. And I can know that my value—which is infinite—is not dependent on anything I am capable of doing. I am liberated from endlessly trying to prove my worth or earn love. I am unworthy, and I am loved beyond measure. This is the paradox of Grace.

The Bible is full of claims that seem at first glance to contradict both themselves and our expectations. Jesus had a particular penchant for paradox. *Whoever finds his life will lose it,* He told the disciples on more than one occasion, *and whoever loses his life for my sake will find it.*[26] If that didn't produce a collective "huh?" from His followers, some of His other statements must have.

Many who are first will be last, and many who are last will be first.[27]

Whoever wants to become great among you must be your servant, and whoever wants to be first must be slave of all.[28]

Blessed are the meek, for they will inherit the earth.[29]

In a society obsessed with power and authority, Jesus' claims must have seemed completely backward in relation to the facts. Undoubtedly some of the people who heard them dismissed them as impractical nonsense. But the ones who followed Jesus began to suggest that the places where faith seemed the most at odds with the prevailing wisdom were keyholes to something beyond reason. The paradoxes were invitations into the Mystery. And the more Christ's followers entered in, the more they became convinced that it was the world that was upside down, and God who was right side up.

Belief did not contradict logic, it both elevated and transcended it. Paradox, after all, was a favorite device of many teachers—a way not of squelching thought but of provoking it and moving it to a higher plane. Jesus was interested in even more than a higher plane, He was introducing a higher *Source*. So with Him the paradox was rather intense. It was foolishness to those who insisted that all the answers began and ended with themselves. But it was life to those who recognized it not only as truth, but as the point of access to a Divine Reason.

I have spent a good deal of my life trying to make the sometimes-cryptic claims of Christianity line up neatly with my thinking. This has been a frustrating and occasionally threatening endeavor. It took several years after my graduation from college for it to dawn on me (courtesy of my producer friend Roy, who rather patiently explained to me a little of the influence of Plato on Western thought) that my reason is not a completely objective, trustworthy instrument of discernment. At least 3000 years of evolving thought and shifting paradigms influence the way I see the world, as do my subjective perceptions, my emotions, and whatever I had for dinner last night. Lately it has occurred to me that rather than wishing Christianity would conform to my way of thinking, it might be more productive for me to realign my way of thinking to Christianity. (Christianity, after all, has remained much more consistent in its claims than Western thought has.) This, I do believe, was at least part of what the apostle Paul was getting at when he urged: "Do not conform any longer to the pattern of this world, but be transformed by the renewing of your mind."[30] The renewing of the mind is not thought's end, but rather its redemption—the beginning of knowledge and wisdom.

Paradox is often used as another word for mystery, and I suspect that Jesus' use of apparent contradiction was a way of revealing that the human intellect is a dead end if it does not begin and end with the Mystery of God. This is the particular predicament of our fallen state: We are driven by our reason to understand and define all things but lost without the one thing that defies all explanation. The reality of our everyday existence is marked by a similar paradox: Everything in our world is illuminated by the one thing we cannot look at without being blinded. "Like the sun at noonday, mysticism explains everything else by the blaze of its own victorious invisibility," said G.K. Chesterton. "We are conscious of it as of a kind of splendid confusion; it is something both shining and shapeless, at once a blaze and a blur."[31]

Tertullian, trying to comprehend God around the turn of the third century, admitted, "I believe because it is absurd." Almost 2000 years later, I find myself coming to much the same conclusion. The fact that Christianity is, at its source, a mystery, is one of the primary proofs we have that we didn't make it up. If we had, we would have fabricated something much more "rational"—something that could be more easily perceived with mortal eyes. All the apparent contradictions and paradoxes that riddle the Bible and our encounters with God are really not threats to faith. They are the beginnings of it.

My heart used to pound with fear when I encountered something I didn't understand in the doctrines of Christianity. These days my heart still pounds, but it is more with excitement than dread. When I encounter a paradox, I know I've come across a chance to get a tiny glimpse of the *blaze* and the *blur* that illuminates and clarifies all truth. I've found a keyhole to the Divine. It seems only reasonable to squint inside.

The heart has its reasons of which reason knows nothing. It is the heart which perceives God and not the reason. That is what faith is: God perceived by the heart, not by the reason.

Blaise Pascal

The best is perhaps what we understand the least.

C.S. Lewis

14

The Bargain

(the meek shall inherit the earth)

Sometime in the early 1980s, my father announced at dinner that he would be selling our blue four-door Impala. It was a momentous decision, and the entire family was very excited by the news. The most spectacular part was my father's promise that, provided he got a good price for the old car, he was going to go out and buy another vehicle— *brand-new, right off the lot*. He placed an ad in the local paper, and we all started hoping and praying for a cooperative buyer. I had not yet heard the saying: *Be careful what you pray for.*

The ad had only been out a few days when a man called to say he'd be very interested in having a look at the car. My dad invited him to come over early that evening. The Impala was parked in the street in front of the house, so my brothers and I determined there would be a pretty good view of the proceedings from the bay window in the living room. The three of us were lined up as inconspicuously as possible on the living room couch when the man arrived.

He seemed decent enough, open-faced and unassuming, and he brought his family—a jumbly brood of giddy kids and an only slightly harried-looking wife. They came spilling up the front walk to our house, but my father headed outside before they reached the front door. The grown-ups shook hands while the kids bounced around them in anticipation.

My brothers and I tried to assess the prospective buyers from our lookout on the couch. The entire family was dressed in clean but threadbare clothing. One of the boys was in a pair of shorts that were obviously too big for him, cinched up at the waist with a belt that was tied in front like a rope. Two of the other children had clearly outgrown their jackets; their skinny arms extended like pipe cleaners past the cuffs of their sleeves. One could only assume that the family's hand-me-down system had fallen a little out of sync with each child's rate of growth. It seemed that maybe they weren't rich.

From the way the family approached the car, you might have thought it was the Holy Grail. They circled around it reverently—from our vantage point it appeared they might actually be *oohing* and *aahing*—and even when the boy in the gunnysack shorts kicked a front tire he did it with respectful restraint. We saw the man ask our dad something—our father nodded and handed him the keys. The entire family jumped into the Impala while the man started the engine, and then the car began to slowly roll down the street. They couldn't have been going more than 15 miles an hour, but as they drove off we saw the ecstatic faces of two of the children pressed against the backseat window. They were wild-eyed and grinning, as if they were heading up Space Mountain rather than around the block.

My father came back up to the house rather nonchalantly, but when he stepped inside the front door his excitement was visible. "They're *really* interested. I'm pretty sure they're going to buy it." My brothers and I started to gleefully debate the make of our brand-new car. After only a few minutes, the Impala came creeping back up to the front of the house. We scrambled back to the couch as our father headed outside.

The kids poured out of the car and stood vibrating together in a nervous huddle. The man and my father began to talk. They kept turning to face the car, so we couldn't read their lips. The conversation seemed to be taking a long time—our tension was mounting. My dad was shaking his head, and then he walked back towards the house. No money had changed hands. Our hearts began to sink.

"Joy!" my father hollered, summoning my mother from the kitchen. "We have a problem." My mom met him in the front hall. "Don't they want it?" she asked, sounding as dejected as we felt. "No, they want it," my dad replied tensely, and he started shaking his head again. "They want to pay what I asked for it in the newspaper. That's way too much!"

My brothers and I were incredulous. Our father was upset because his buyer wanted to give him *too much money?* It didn't seem possible. This was the same man we had seen haggle relentlessly for better deals with everyone he'd ever done business with. We'd watched him bring Tijuana leather and pottery vendors to their knees. He was a banker. He liked to save and earn money. It was his sport. What was going on?

"They're supposed to *negotiate,*" my father said petulantly. My mother thought for a minute. "Tell them the AM radio doesn't work, so you're taking off 200 dollars," she suggested. My father looked relieved. He went back outside.

My mother returned to the kitchen. My brothers and I sank back onto the couch and watched, stunned, as our dad went on a mission to talk his buyer into a lower price. The man's wife was holding her youngest child on her hip, leaning lightly against the hood of the car, gesturing to the other kids to stay out of the street. My father talked with the man and woman for a couple of minutes. Then he turned on his heel and strode purposefully back up to the house. We still hadn't seen any cash.

"Joy," called my dad as he came through the door. She reemerged from the kitchen. "Did you reduce the price?" she asked, the beginnings of a smile tugging at her lips. "Yes," he said with a sigh of exasperation, "but it's still too much. I really don't think they can afford it. And I've just found out they're *missionaries* up north, for crying out loud. They're so excited because they'll be able to use the car to drive families back and forth to Sunday school." By this point in his monologue, my father had begun to appear a little desperate. He was pacing across the tiles in the entrance way, and there was sweat on his forehead. "Joy," he said, an edge of panic in his voice, "they think the Impala is the most amazing car they've ever seen because it has electric windows."

My mom was laughing, just a little, very gently. She kissed my father on the cheek. "Tell them one of the air vents is blocked. And we don't know where the passenger-side floor mat is. Take off as much as you want, honey." My father nodded, raising his head and straightening his back a little, happy to have the weight off his shoulders. He headed back outside.

There was a mild argument—the man no doubt trying to talk my father into a higher price. After a few minutes of discussion, the man pulled out his wallet (*finally!*) and handed my father some cash. My father did not even count it. The man grabbed my father's hand and shook it enthusiastically. The kids began arguing about who was going to go home in the wreck they had come in, and who would get to ride in their "new" Impala. My father strolled back up the porch steps, looking just as delighted as he had the time he got three huge Mexican flowerpots for 70 percent off. "They love the car," he said, beaming his way into the house. "To them it's a Cadillac. Better than a Cadillac. It's like the Bond car or something." We turned back to the window as the family floated away in a two-car parade. And even as we watched our brand-new, right-off-the-lot vehicle drive away with them, my parents and my brothers were grinning from ear to ear, and I'm pretty sure I was too.

When Jesus proclaimed that the meek would inherit

the earth, I'm certain He was thinking of something a bit more expansive than a great deal on a used Impala. As best as I can understand it, He was revealing how radically different God's priorities are from our priorities. We think the meek are weak. He thinks the meek are blessed. We think you have to fight to get anything in this world. He wishes we'd stop fighting long enough to receive everything He has to give. And part of what He wants to give is an eternal inheritance, a place in His kingdom.

It is one thing to understand Jesus' statement as a prophetic promise; it is another, more difficult thing to believe it expresses any sort of present reality in the physical world. The essence of meekness is humility, gentleness, and submission to God. In this earthly economy, humility, gentleness, and submissiveness are considered liabilities. And yet, ever since the night we sold the Impala, I have had the sneaking suspicion that—in some intangible but wonderful way—sometimes the meek really do inherit the earth in the here and now. Three hundred years ago, Matthew Henry gave this phenomenon the best explanation I have found.

> *[The meek] are in the least danger of being injured and disturbed in the possession of what they have and they have most satisfaction in themselves and consequently the sweetest relish of their creature-comforts....Perhaps they have not abundance of wealth to delight in; but they have that which is better, abundance of peace, inward peace and tranquility of mind, peace with God, and then peace in God, that great*

peace which those have that love God's law, whom nothing
shall offend.[32]

I don't know a lot about the family that "inherited"
my father's car (by the time he was done negotiating, my dad
had pretty much given away the Impala), but I can make
some educated guesses. I wouldn't be surprised to learn they
were living below the poverty line, and I can easily imagine
some of their old high school friends discussing them with
bewilderment. *I don't know what went wrong with those guys. Last I*
heard they were living up north, with all those kids, flat broke, preaching
or something. Of course, all I really know for sure is that they
were missionaries, and they were a little naive, and they lived
simply and humbly enough to think our crummy old Impala
was utterly fabulous. They seemed happy to me, and it
looked as though they loved each other, but I don't have
enough information to be able to make any sweeping, conclusive statements about the blessings of their meek existence. What I *can* say with certainty is that for at least that
mild summer night, slowly lowering the electric windows as
they drove away in their fabulous new Impala, they had the
world on a string. And the funny thing is, when I remember
my dad whistling his way through the rest of that evening, I
realize that he did too.

He has showed you, O man, what is good. And what does the LORD require of you? To act justly and to love mercy and to walk humbly with your God.

Micah 6:8

For the Lord takes delight in his people; he crowns the humble with salvation. Let the saints rejoice in this honor and sing for joy on their beds.

Psalm 149:4-5

15

Jump Shots and Salchows

(strength in weakness)

Early in my music career, just after the release of my first album, Rich Mullins asked me if I'd like to go out on the road as one of his opening acts on a three-month tour. I said yes.

I was awkward around Rich, awestruck in the presence of one of my heroes, intimidated by his intensity, a little disoriented by the rougher edges I hadn't expected. He was aggressively friendly, badgering me to read a rather lengthy list of his favorite books, demanding we all join him on side trips to divers' cliffs and Mexican restaurants and Appalachian music shops. If he found something he loved, he wanted rather desperately for his friends to discover it too. He drank up life in great, lusty gulps, and passed the cup around to the rest of us.

In many ways Rich was an open book. He certainly felt that everyone was entitled to his opinion, and it wasn't hard to tell whether something struck him as hilarious or horrific or just plain boring. But for some reason I never really felt I knew him that well. He seemed to me to be a complicated soul—a brilliant, disheveled mass of contradictions. Some of the people who were close to him have called him transparent—to me his transparency was like the clear water I used to stare into at the inlet by our house. On a calm day, when you could see right through the water to the ocean floor, you realized that underneath that transparent liquid was a complex labyrinth of barnacles and seaweed and whatever other things grow in deep waters. Rich was never particularly still, but I knew he ran deep, and I was often baffled by him.

Looking back, I can see I probably would have gotten to know Rich better if I had been more real with him. I was constantly surprised by him—sometimes he would utter something so profound I knew instinctively it would stay with me the rest of my life, and in the next breath he would say something so ridiculous or intentionally offensive I would nearly fall off my chair. But I never called him on it— never told him when I thought he was being absurd, never thanked him when I knew he was changing my life. I was too cautious around him. Maybe without realizing it I was put off a little by his lack of pretense. A polite, Canadian Baptist girl like me enjoys her reality in small and polished doses—with Rich I found myself in a state of overload.

There was a night, however, when the sudden discovery of a commonality between us vaporized my hesitancy and awkwardness for a while. I was idling backstage over the obligatory tins of warmed-up lasagna and defrosted vegetables—the preconcert dinner. Rich wandered in from a run, windblown and sweaty and relaxed. I made some comment admiring his commitment to his daily jog and confessed my complete ineptitude when it comes to sports of any variety. Rich laughed and dragged a plastic chair up next to me. "Sports," he said, with a certain amount of disdain. "Try growing up in Indiana and hating basketball."

To hear Rich tell it, an inability or disinterest in basketball was—for Hoosiers—the one Unforgivable Sin, and he was guilty of it. He knew from an early age he wasn't going to be a contender, so he pulled himself out of the game, bitterly disappointing his father (or so it seemed to him at the time), and leaving Rich with a sense of being a little on the outside of things. That alienation, he claimed, stayed with him throughout his high school years. I was surprised by the edge of resentment in his voice, startled to realize that an old teenage wound was still tender in the famously successful man before me. But I could relate.

Perhaps the only thing worse than poor basketball skills in Indiana is the complete inability to skate in Canada. I got my first set of stiff white figure skates when I was six.

I'm not sure, but I think if the Canadian government had seen me flailing about the local ice rink they may have stripped me of my citizenship. The more determined I was to learn, the more abysmal I became. My parents kept shelling out the lesson fees, and I kept falling and catching colds and trying to figure out what was wrong with my skates—they just didn't work properly.

Those chilly, futile lessons were successful in only one respect—they encouraged the blossoming imagination (some might call it a "fantasy world," but I prefer to think of it as a "rich interior life") that I still rely on to this day. I began developing a scenario in my mind. I was not really a terrible skater at all—on the contrary, I was a world-famous gold-medallist cleverly disguised as an uncoordinated seven year old. The Canadian Figure Skating Federation had secretly hired me to test the quality of the public lesson system. Although it was completely contrary to my innate athleticism, I had to masquerade as an inexperienced skater so I wouldn't blow my cover. As I wobbled and crashed my way across the treacherous ice, I smiled covertly to myself. When the assignment was finally over, I would launch into an exquisitely executed triple salchow, finally revealing my true identity to my stunned teachers and the wildly enthusiastic crowd.

My forays into other sports continued to nurture my interior life as I approached the minefield of adolescence. For some reason my softball coach played me almost exclusively in right field, so I had plenty of time to dream up stories and songs and plans to save the world while the Saturday sun turned me freckled and brown. My reverie was seldom broken, although occasionally some superhuman opponent would actually hit the ball far enough to reach me. Despite my best attempts to evade it, the ball would inevitably bounce off the tip of my glove and smash its way into my face—leaving the imprint of my braces on the insides of my lips and the taste of blood in my mouth. There would be a brief jumble of confusion as I scrambled after the ball and threw it in the general direction of the infield. But it was never long before I was left to my imagination once again.

I was tall enough to make the grade eight basketball team and soon discovered my lack of ball control was surpassed only by the inaccuracy of my shot. So I moved on to girl's field hockey a sport not suitable for the faint of heart or tender of shin. I did manage to score the one and only goal of the muddy season (I kid you not, the *entire* team scored only once the *entire* season)—the crowning achievement of my high school athletic career. By grade eleven I had hung up my sneakers for good (except, unfortunately, for mandated physical education classes) and embraced the worlds of books and music with all of my uncoordinated heart.

When Rich talked about being an outsider in a hoops-crazed world, I required no further explanation. I know how it feels to hold down the bench, to be picked last (grudgingly) for the schoolyard teams. But I was curious about something. "Were you already into music back then?" I asked him. Rich grinned. "Yep." He proceeded to tell me how his family marked the milestone of a certain age (I forget now if it was 13 or 16 or some other year) with the gift of a cow. Each child anxiously awaited the appropriate birthday, and then promptly sold the cow and bought a car or some other equally desired treasure. Rich bought a piano.

I saw Rich Mullins perform 63 times on that 3-month tour, and not once was I left unmoved. What struck me most was his ability to connect almost instantly with the disenfranchised, the alienated, and the marginalized—with anybody who had ever felt left out—which is to say, with everybody. For who among us has lived this life without sometimes feeling apart or alone? I am rather selfishly thankful that Rich was forced a little to the outside of things as a young man, because I suspect his wonderfully skewed view of life (not to mention his keen awareness that we are strangers and aliens in this world) would not have developed any other way. Standing just left of center, he saw piercingly into the middle of human experience, and he began to describe it in wise and funny and poetic and prophetic ways. All those hours he could have poured into shooting hoops he spent pounding on his piano, enfleshing in melody and lyrics the things we have all felt but struggled to express.

Already I have begun to pray with great fervor that my hockey-crazed, two-year-old little boy turns out to be a fine, strong skater...and that he's a confident, successful student, and does well in piano lessons, and always gets invited to dances, and never feels stupid or uncool or alone. It makes me feel sick to my stomach to know that not all of these prayers will be answered in the affirmative—that there will be days he cries hot tears of rejection just as surely as I did and do and will continue to do. I imagine that in those moments I will remind him that God loves him just the way he is. If I'm feeling particularly inspired I may even tell him about my old friend Rich, whose exceptional gifting could be attributed—at least a little—to his weak shot from the free throw line.

"When I am weak, then I am strong," the apostle Paul was fond of saying. Life has taught me that lesson well—it takes painful confrontations with my own inadequacy and brokenness and aloneness to make me realize how much I need the help and wholeness and belongingness that only a relationship with God can bring. But I am beginning to think there is even more to this paradox of strength in weakness. I love the fact that Jesus chose the salty apostle Peter—a guy whose big mouth got him into all kinds of trouble his whole life—as the cornerstone of His church, confident that the mysterious machinations of grace would transform Peter's tendency to blurt things out into a great gift for proclaiming the truth.

In the last-shall-be-first kingdom of forgiveness and mercy, our deepest inadequacies are not only accepted, they become our assets. We expect a God of power to obliterate our weaknesses—instead we are more likely to encounter a God of love who finds impossibly creative ways to convert those liabilities into our best features. Only the Author of love could come up with a plot twist like this in the story of redemption—we actually become better not in spite of, but *because* of, our infirmities.

Perhaps it was Beethoven's physical deafness that enabled him to hear—uninterrupted—the glorious themes of his Ninth Symphony. Or Milton's blindness that intensified his vivid interior vision of *Paradise Lost*. Could the poet Blake have given us the fearful symmetry of his "Lamb" and "Tyger" with a less troubled mind? The great novelist Dostoyevsky claimed that his extraordinary insights were somehow connected to his epilepsy. And what of the apostle Paul—could he have taught all the believers after him that suffering leads to perseverance, character, and, ultimately, hope if his pesky thorn had been removed?

This is another part of what it is to enter into the Mystery—to discover that wherever our greatest brokenness lies, there also lies our greatest potential. These transformations are not easy—the truth is they are often excruciatingly slow and painful. But they are real nonetheless—or at least they can be if we give every aspect of ourselves to our Maker to be recreated. This, I believe, was something Rich Mullins understood, and it gave him wholeness and wild hope and irrepressible joy. I should not have been surprised to find contradiction and complexity in a man who embraced mystery and paradox and knew himself to be in the middle of a long-term reconstruction—a man somewhat impatiently awaiting the total redemption of the best and worst of himself. Though now he is gone from us—his transformation complete—he has left us a few hundred melodies and lyrics that document a heart given over to believing and questioning and diving deeper into the Mystery...songs that demand, with typical Mullins' passion, that we do the same and be forever changed.

My grace is enough; it's all you need.

My strength comes into its own in your weakness.

1 Corinthians 12:9 (MSG)

16

The
Donation

(lose your life to find it)

Rich always said that of all the songs he'd written, his
favorite was "Elijah." *When I leave I want to go out like
Elijah*, he used to sing with his trademark Mullins' grin, *and
it won't break my heart to say goodbye.*[33] In a strange way, he got
his wish—when his Jeep of a chariot left the ground, Rich
was gone in an instant. After he died, and the awful shock of
it started to wear off a little, many of us who had loved him
and his music began to notice how often he had talked and
sung about his own death. "Do you think he *knew?*" we

would ask each other, usually with a bit of a shiver.

As I write this, I consider for the first time the slightly eerie significance of Rich's great love for John Irving's *A Prayer for Owen Meany*—the funny and ultimately heartbreaking story of a boy who had a premonition in which he saw his own tombstone and some of the tragic details of his eventual death. When Rich was encouraging me (ordering me, really) to read the book, he told me that anyone who did was instantly inducted into a secret Owen Meany Society. He claimed a simple recitation of the novel's last sentence could bring tears to the eyes of any club member. He was right, and the tears come now as I remember the prayer that ends the story. *O God—please give him back! I shall keep asking you.*[34]

Of course, none of us can say if Rich really had any sense that his life would be shorter than most. But the more I remember about the way he lived his 41 years on this planet, the more I think that Rich simply understood and embraced something most of us expend a good deal of energy trying to deny—the fact that life is fatal. We're all terminal. Whether we get 40 or 80 years to spend on this earth, it amounts to roughly the blink of an eye in the course of even temporal history, let alone in the eternal scheme of things. Most of us are so horribly afraid of our inevitable fate that we become more engaged in avoiding our deaths than we do in living our lives. I think this is at least one of the reasons we are so obsessed with youth in our culture—the signs of aging in our own bodies and in the faces of the people we love sound off death-bell alarms that we'll do anything not to hear. We are grateful for any distraction that might help us forget the end of the story.

But Rich's life encompassed yet another paradox—he believed the end was the beginning. He was convinced that God had prepared a place for him, a city where he could talk face-to-face with Elijah and Moses, Abraham and Jacob. A land where at long last he could see and be with Jesus. Heaven. Rich's conviction that an eternal life was waiting did not diminish his love for his earthly existence—if anything, it intensified it. It made him fearless and free. He didn't waste a lot of energy trying to convince himself that life is longer than it really is. He enjoyed every fleeting second for the precious, fragile gift that it was. And so he spent his time here not as a fatalist but as an adventurer—his life less a mortal coil than a sacred journey.

If you had only 24 hours to live, how would you spend them? I am often asked in interviews (a question only slightly less popular than *If you were a tree, what kind of tree would you be?*). It's not hard to answer. I don't think there's much I would *do*—maybe make sure I was wearing nice underwear in case my death involved a visit to the hospital or some other equally revealing chain of events. No doubt I would call my family and my friends and express the love and gratitude I so often leave unspoken. I would want to reconcile any unresolved relationships, and I am sure I would urge the people I love who have not yet embraced faith to investigate Jesus.

But I think I would spend most of my last few hours just *being*—loving my husband and son, drinking them in and trying to pour out for them whatever it is that I am, hoping to give them my essence to remember me by. I would hold back nothing. And I imagine that with the awareness that I was soon to breathe my last would come enough freedom from distraction to finally be still and know that God was God. More than anything else, I would seek His presence, and I would not rest until I knew I was at peace with Him.

It is my sincere hope that I presently have quite a bit more than 24 hours left, but it's a safe bet that in even the most optimistic scenario I don't have more than 50 or 60 years. The first 32 have flown by, and time seems to be picking up speed—any way you look at it, I really don't have long to live. In the few brave and lucid moments I actually let that reality sink in, my priorities are almost entirely reversed. I want to spend more time being than I spend doing and reacting. I want to hold nothing back—after all, what am I saving it for? A wonderful mass of humanity has been placed in my life—family and friends and neighbors and colleagues and church members and incidental passersby. I want to love them out loud, now, instead of storing it all up for some eventual regret-filled deathbed confession. And more than anything else I want to make seeking peace with God the supreme quest of every moment.

I want to live like I would if I had only one more day.

———————

A while ago I found myself standing in an exceedingly long line at the LA airport. From my vantage point I could not even see the ticket counter. An impatient throng of perspiring travelers stood between me and my flight, and the line was barely moving. Every five minutes or so, we would collectively inch forward like an extremely lethargic snake, and I would have to wrestle and kick my cumbersome luggage ever-so-slightly ahead.

Behind me was a man in a fresh tan, Bermuda shorts, and a "Belize" T-shirt. He was swearing with considerable skill—combining cuss words into inventive phrases I had not previously heard, cursing God as if He was the one running the airline. He was frustrated that there were not more agents working at the counter, furious at the lack of service on his previous flight, and, right at the moment, incensed at the world. I nodded sympathetically a few times, but I mostly tried to keep my head down and stay out of his way.

In my efforts to avoid making eye contact with the man (I learned from the Nature Channel never to return the stare of an enraged predator), I was gazing absently in the general direction of the escalators. Gradually, a woman began to come into focus. She was wearing a crisp, white dress and cap that resembled an old-fashioned nurse's uniform, except that there were red-and-gold military-like embellishments on the shoulders. Her dark hair was swept up in an immaculate bun. She looked weary but not drawn, and though she may have been fifty her almond skin was stretched smoothly across her broad face. Every few minutes she would shift her weight from one orthopedic shoe to the other—it appeared as though she'd been standing there a while. In front of her was a donation ball, similar to the ones the Salvation Army hauls out at Christmas time, and it contained a rather pitiful quantity of loose change. She was holding a sign that read: *Support missions and drug rehabilitations centers…Say "no" to drugs, say "yes" to Jesus.*

As people streamed by to get off and on the elevators, she would look directly at them and speak very gently in either English or Spanish, depending on their apparent nationality. Hardly anyone returned her gaze or even acknowledged she was there. She did not appear discouraged, but I was moved with compassion for her. I would not want to be the one standing in her sensible shoes.

I pulled a few dollars from my wallet, but something kept me from walking over to her. I wondered if she really represented a nonprofit agency—there were occasional announcements over the loudspeaker warning airport patrons not to give money to unauthorized solicitors. But there was an official LAX identification badge clipped onto her right sleeve, complete with photograph. And airport security personnel were passing by her with no apparent concerns. I decided she was probably there on behalf of a legitimate organization.

But I still didn't go over to her, and I am embarrassed to admit now it was because I was afraid of what the man in the sweaty Belize T-shirt would think. No doubt he would be disgusted at my naiveté, skeptical that a donation would do anything other than encourage the panhandler problem in Los Angeles. The mood he was in, he might even say something about it, and I would be mortified. I was annoyed at my own timidity, but I was on the final leg of a long journey, and I really wasn't up for any sort of tense confrontation. So I stuffed the money in my pocket, and I told myself that if there was time I would go back to the escalators and make a donation after I'd checked in for my flight.

I'd been smiling at the lady occasionally, but now I felt a little too ashamed to meet her eyes. I was also still trying to avoid the stare of the man behind me, so I pretty much had no option but to look at my feet. The line continued to crawl forward, and as we snaked past the lady with the sign, I reprised my interior debate one more time. *Come on*, I scolded myself. *Where's your spine?* Before I could determine the answer to my question, something rather unexpected happened. The angry man behind me stepped out of the line, walked over to the woman, handed her a nice little bundle of bills, and said with a sympathetic smile, "Take it easy."

I felt extraordinarily foolish; a hot blush was creeping across my face. *Great*, I thought, *now when I donate he's going to think I'm just copying him.* This, of course, was a new height of stupidity, which I recognized instantly, thank goodness. I went over to the woman, and I dug the money out of my pocket and gave it to her. As she thanked me she looked directly into my eyes in a way that made me feel she knew entirely too much about me. "God bless you," she said.

I think I remember that moment so distinctly because it reminded me of who I am meant to be. If I would go with the purer instincts of my heart, I would give whatever I could whenever I could, whether it made a lot of sense or not. If I would listen to the better angels of my nature, I would meet the gaze of the lady by the escalators, and, for that matter, the hungover guy on the street and the frustrated traveler standing next to me in line. I would be the first to say, "God bless you," instead of the last. That's the sort of life I was meant to have, the existence I will be most happy living. But to have that life, I have to give up some of the things that characterize my life now—the concern over what other people will think, the self-protective cautiousness, the reserve that keeps me from being fully engaged. Quite frankly, I have to get over myself in order to find myself.

Whoever finds his life will lose it, Jesus said, *and whoever loses his life for my sake will find it.*[35] He was no doubt expressing the secret of eternal life—in some mysterious way we are to actually die with Christ in order to share in His resurrection. But Jesus had a way of saying things that are true in an infinite number of directions and applications, and His words also expose the secrets to living the kind of life most of us want to have here on earth. *Lose your life to find it. Get over yourself. Live every day like it's your last. Hold nothing back. And, for heaven's sake, try not to go through airports staring at your feet.*

We are here to love. And the enemy of love is self-consciousness.

Tom Jackson

17

Dreams of Kings and Carpenters

(the Incarnation)

Of all the paradoxes in the New Testament, there is one more impossible than all the others, and the contradiction is not in something Jesus says but in what He *is*...fully God and fully man, together. A crazy (and ultimately violent) collision of human and holy, somehow contained in ordinary flesh and bone. It is the Mystery of Mysteries, and it starts with—of all things—a baby.

This past December Mark and I went with our friends Nikki and John to see *Dreams of Kings and Carpenters*,[36] a strange and beautiful play produced by Pacific Theatre in Vancouver. I was suffering from "Christmas angst"—the guilty awareness that I was not so much celebrating the advancing Advent season as panicking over the decreasing number of remaining shopping days. I thought maybe a good old-fashioned Christmas production could help clear my head and realign my heart.

The play was more than I had bargained for. There were no familiar, benign, bathrobed shepherds or towel-turbaned wise men. We were confronted instead with the pathos, humor, romance, and danger of a truth much stranger than fiction. There was Mary—pregnant out of wedlock and offering in all seriousness the most absurd explanation imaginable. And there was Joseph—broken-hearted and ready to break the neck of whoever had taken advantage of the girl he loved. There was an angel too, of course, faced with the daunting task of convincing Joseph that his dream really was a message from God and that Mary's story was just crazy enough to be true.

The action happened in fragments—snatches of dialogue and song—and each member of the small cast appeared as more than one character in the drama. We recognized grizzled old Simeon sitting at the temple, staring intensely at the happy young parents who brought their babies to the priest, and we knew he was waiting to see if God would make good on His promise to let him see the Christ-child. When the play asked us to imagine what might have motivated his daily visits to the temple, we were surprised by the bitterness in his voice as he revealed his longing for the wife he had lost and the child

God had never given them. And then we laughed as Zechariah—recently struck dumb as a temporary punishment for his disbelief—used a writing tablet and some very creative sign language to convince his Elizabeth that God had made a ridiculous, wonderful decision to grow a new life in her barren old womb.

But Mary and Joseph remained the heart of the story, and the drama always found its way back to them. We were relieved when they reconciled, delighted when they embraced. It was impossible not to be drawn into their journey as they walked—expectant and weary—toward Bethlehem.

We were permitted a view of the stable, and though we felt a bit embarrassed by our intrusion, we could not tear our eyes away from the intimate and holy scene. The stage grew dark and the actors began to describe the messy, painful business of Mary's labor in tense, vivid poetry:

> *Blood-strewn straw…*
> *Father be with us in the ripping dark.*[37]

And then—just when it was almost unbearable—the baby arrived, and the voices whispered together:

> *He comes.*
> *Love's bloom, bright and wild.*[38]

Mary, regaining her strength, gasped, *Unto us a child is born…*to which Joseph, his heart in his throat, replied, *Unto us a son is given.*[39]

Act I was over and, mercifully, there was an intermission. Mark and I squinted at our friends in the bright lights of the lobby and struggled for words. "You like it so far?"

"Yes," said Nikki. "Definitely," said John. And then we all just stood there—reverent and emotional and more than a little dazed.

I had come looking for an opportunity to restore my sense of wonder, to rediscover the Mystery that I had almost forgotten existed in the midst of my Christmas rush. *Dreams of Kings and Carpenters* brought me back to the manger and laid out the miracle for my inspection. When the baby came I remembered that Mary's child was the prince of *my* peace and the light of *my* world. At last I was ready for Christmas.

But there was a second act to the play, and things started to go seriously awry. Just before the lights dimmed, I noticed that the playbill indicated that the actress who played Elizabeth would also be playing a character named Rachel. My heart sank like a rock. I knew what was coming. *Rachel weeping for her children, and refusing to be comforted, because they are no more.*[40] The play had just given us a breathtaking picture of the miracle of the Incarnation. Surely they weren't going to ruin a perfectly inspiring evening with such a tragic twist. The idea of describing the birth of Christ and the slaughter of Bethlehem innocents in the same breath seemed obscene.

It *is* obscene, of course, but it is also part of the story. And so, act 2 told us not only of wise men but of the insecure king who employed them. There were armies of angels, to be sure, full of joy and such intensity of life that the glory of the Lord shone round about them. *Do not be afraid!* But there were also armies of the ordinary kind—young soldiers, trained to intimidate and kill and do what must be done in the name of Political Necessity. "Keeping the peace," they called it. *Be afraid.*

Dreams of Kings and Carpenters invited us to imagine what it might have been like to be a citizen of Bethlehem 2000 years ago—to hear and maybe even half-believe the wild rumors of angels appearing to common shepherds and the long-awaited Messiah wriggling His way out into a barn. After a while, would the rumors die down? Would we think it had all been a crazy dream when our impoverished, oppressed lives continued on much as they had before— worse, maybe, than they had been before?

Just as I feared, the play introduced us to a girl named Rachel, and she was rocking her son to sleep with the tender and ferocious love that consumes young mothers. She was talking with a friend, describing with a conflicted mix of skepticism and wonder and desperate hope the night she had seen angels (of all things!) and met another young mother named Mary. Squirming in my seat, I started to hear the strange static that roars in my ears when the sudden threat of danger appears. The appropriate responses are Fight or Flight, but I could do neither.

The play continued, and Joseph opted for Flight, because the angel warned him to take Mary and the baby and run to Egypt (by this time Joseph and the angel had gotten to know each other pretty well). It was no longer safe in Bethlehem because King Herod was not happy about the idea of some would-be Messiah in diapers usurping his authority. He ordered the slaughter of every baby boy under the age of two in the vicinity of Bethlehem. If the soldiers were trained in anything, it was in following orders. So they did.

And then Rachel was weeping for her child, because he was no more.

I wept too. I was thinking, of course, of my 22-month-old blessing of a boy, safe at home with the sitter. I was also thinking of the sweet friends sitting next to me. Nicole and John are good, honest people who approach the world with open hearts and open hands and a sturdy, well-used faith. Nikki's belly was already beginning to swell with their own miracle—a baby due in May. But their first child—a child they had prayed for through a struggle with infertility—had died before they ever got a chance to see its precious face. After the miscarriage, the doctors said it had been something called a "pregnancy mole"—they never really clarified whether the baby my friends had loved desperately and thanked and praised God for had ever really been a baby at all.

From the stage, Rachel was crying the question.

> *Why, God? You opened my womb and gave me a son.*
> *I was thankful then. Every mother would be. But why*
> *give me a son, only to take him away?*
>
> *...Answer me, Lord. Answer me. I am waiting for an*
> *answer.*[41]

I was waiting for an answer, too, and the question belonged not only to Rachel, and to Nikki and John, but to anyone who has ever wondered why God steps into history to give us His Son but does nothing when the people we love are taken away too early or too cruelly. Why miscarriage? Why cancer? Why war? Why infertility? Why car accidents? Why are thousands massacred? Why is one child beaten? Why?

The play, maddeningly, left the question hanging. We returned to Simeon, still at the temple, but no longer waiting. Mary and Joseph had brought little Jesus to the priest, and Simeon had at last heard God's voice. *That's the one.* And then Mary had let him hold the Messiah.

I feel like dancing, Simeon said. He hauled himself up on his cane and careened about the stage while the cast sang a boisterous "Joy to the World." There were audible sighs in the audience, a grateful release of tension.

But before we could get too relaxed or relieved, the stage emptied of everyone but Joseph, and we eavesdropped as the carpenter dreamed about his son's future.

> *Just wait till we get back to Nazareth.*
> *I'll teach you everything I know.*
> *...You will bear the pungent smell of new wood*
> *and wear shavings and sawdust in your hair.*
>
> *You'll be a man whose life centers*
> *on hammer and nails and wood.*
> *But for now,*
> *sleep, little Jesus, sleep.*[42]

The play was over. We exploded in applause—thankful for the gift we had been given. Christmas. Beautiful, but messy and complicated too. Just the sort of thing needed to redeem our messy, complicated lives, I suppose.

We said goodbye to Nikki and John and the baby in Nikki's tummy. Then we drove home, anxious to see our boy. He was already asleep, but we stood over his crib for a few moments anyway, and I couldn't stop myself from touching his tousled blond hair. Christmas was going to be so fun this year. Already, Ben was ecstatic over the lights on the houses and the tree in our living room. Mark took my hand in the dark and we tiptoed out of Ben's room. My heart was full.

But Rachel's question was still left hanging, and that night my full heart and my heavy head got into an argument. I knew Joseph's final words had hinted at Jesus' fate, so in a sense, the play left Him hanging too. But I also knew that three days after He was nailed to a cross, Jesus got up, walked out of His grave, and conquered death once and for all. Still, the questions were only intensified in the blazing light of the resurrection. If death has been defeated, why is this whole earthly existence so characterized by it? Why is death the one thing we can count on?

I found myself in a familiar place that December night—once again demanding answers I simply am not capable of understanding, seeking knowledge I probably could not bear to know. A finite creature railing at heaven's door, failing to grasp the infinite. The Divine Frustration. Again.

And then I was struck for the first time by something that really should have been obvious. The Incarnation shows us clearly that the Divine Frustration works both ways. An infinite God, seeking to love and be known by His finite creations, finally resorts to His only option. All we can comprehend is the finite, so He comes up with a drastic, desperate, radical plan to make Himself finite. He sends His Son. He places His unfathomable power into the most powerless form there is—a newborn. And even though He knows how the story ends—His Son despised, rejected, forced to suffer the greatest sorrow ever endured—He is so glad to finally be offering His creation a chance to know Him that He actually celebrates. He has His angels sing.

> *I bring you good news of great joy that will be for all the people. Today in the town of David a Savior has been born to you: he is Christ the Lord.*[43]

The story sometimes gives me the strangest picture of God the Father looking down at the nativity scene—our whole planet roughly the size of a snow globe—with a sort of Divine satisfaction. *It is good*, He says, echoing His words from the dawn of creation, pleased at having finally provided a way for us to be reconciled to Him. The baby sleeps.

And then the baby grows up and lives among the Nazarenes—we know this, it is historical fact. When He is roughly my age, He tells those close to Him, *Greater love has no one than this, that he lay down his life for his friends.*[44] On a hill called Calvary, He shows them what He means. And again I see God the Father looking down on the scene, but this time it's too awful, and for a moment He has to look away. Maybe He does not say *It is good*, but His Son says *It is finished*. And they both consider it a sacrifice worth making.

In Christ, God reveals to us the aspects of Himself He most urgently wants us to see. More than anything else He shows us love. Awful, wonderful, powerful love. The curtain in the temple is torn in two by this love. The great divide between God and man is crossed by this love. There is no greater love than this—Jesus laying down His life so that we might become the friends of God.

If this is the whole quest of God—that we should love Him as He loves us, that we should become His friends—we must be free to reject His offer. This is a terrible freedom, and I suspect it is at the heart of most of the terrors in this world. We cannot love God unless we are free not to love Him. Many of us don't. He does not override our wills. He does not move us about like pawns in a cosmic chess game, always ensuring an agreeable outcome. We are free to bring hate into the world (and indifference too, which is really hate in its most lethal form), and so we bring also disease and pollution and crime and death. If God were to force us to stop the hate, He would eliminate the opportunity for us to choose love.

Someday, He *will* stop the whole enterprise. His Son will return and this world as we know it will be no more. Until then, He is—for lack of a better word—a gentleman. He steps into history, He moves in our world, but only where there is a Mary willing to say *I am the Lord's servant* or a Joseph who can be convinced that an angel is really an angel and not just the product of wishful thinking. Now that Jesus is once again at the right hand of the Father, we are asked to be not His mother and father but His hands and feet. He will not force Himself upon us. But if we are willing, He will move through us.

This a paradox perhaps even more mysterious than the Incarnation. God chooses to be incarnated day after day in you and me. But only if we choose to let Him. Because the love freely given at Bethlehem, at Calvary, and wherever you are sitting right this moment must be freely received. Otherwise it isn't love at all. And if the Incarnation tells us anything, it tells us that God is love.

I will confess that I felt a flash of something like resentment when *Dreams of Kings and Carpenters* confronted me with some cruel realities in the midst of a bright and beautiful story. But I am beginning to see that if the story is really true, it must be as true in the thick of soldiers as it is in the company of angels. The Incarnation contains many mysteries, and one of the saddest but most essential mysteries is this: Wherever there is a Rachel weeping for her children, there is a God who understands what it is to lose a beloved child. He is not the source of our suffering, He is its only consolation. And, in the midst of our darkness, He offers the shining hope of a life that conquers even death and a love that can save the world—one willing heart at a time.

The dark riddle of life is illuminated in Jesus.

Brennan Manning

Living the Questions

The anonymous author of **The Cloud of Unknowing** *writes, "By love God may be gotten and holden, but by thought or understanding, never."*

Love, not answers.

Love, which trusts God so implicitly despite the cloud (and is not the cloud a sign of God?), that it is brave enough to ask questions, no matter how fearful.

Madeleine L'Engle

18

Belief and Unbelief

I want the life that conquers death and the love that changes the world more than anything. But why is it that even when my heart and my spirit are willing, it is not only my flesh but my *faith* that is sometimes weak?

There is a story in the Gospel of Mark about a father and his very sick son and the miracle that changes their lives. It turns out to also be a story about belief and unbelief—about faith that survives even its own weakness—and it is probably my favorite miracle story in the Bible.

The son has been afflicted since childhood by a demon that causes seizures, and the illness has become so savagely aggressive that it has robbed him even of the power of speech. We're not given many details, but the few facts that are presented make it obvious that the father is the sort of man who will do anything to help his child. It's only too easy to imagine him lunging at every new medical breakthrough, hoping against hope, only to be disappointed. Maybe he's even become desperate enough to listen to old wives' tales and actually heed superstitions he would have laughed at when he was younger (back when he believed it was a man's hard work and clear conscience that secured him a healthy and happy life). Regardless, nothing works. And now, every time his son is wracked by another convulsion, the father is privately wracked by fear and despair and rage at his own helplessness.

He hears the latest rumors, of course—how could he not? Everyone is buzzing with the news—some of the saddest, most hopeless cases in Tyre and Sidon claim to have been miraculously healed. There is a man named Jesus—some say He is able to cure blindness and paralysis with just a word or a touch. The wildest stories even have Him raising the dead. He's not a doctor, and He doesn't seem to be a shyster, at least not of the normal variety. He charges nothing. But it all sounds a little crazy. Some of His followers claim He is the Jewish Messiah.

I imagine the father telling the boy to get his coat. "Oh, no," says his wife, tears welling up in her weary eyes. "Don't put him through it again. Don't put *us* through it again. Please." The man pauses for a moment, pressing his thumbs against his temples. He sits back down at the kitchen table. She's right, of course. Time to wise up. What does the proverb say? *Hope deferred makes the heart sick.*[45] Better not to hope at all.

A few minutes later the boy is thrown to the ground in a particularly violent seizure. His mother reacts with her usual grim courage and resignation, crying silently as she clears the furniture away from where he lies writhing on the floor. "It'll be all right," she says to no one in particular. Even as the boy continues to flail she reaches out to wipe the foam away from his contorted mouth.

The father stares with renewed horror at the scene before him, and, when the boy finally goes limp, he slams his fist down on the kitchen table. His chair crashes to the ground as he gets up and scoops his son into his arms in one swift motion. "I've *got* to go," he says, not looking at his wife. "God knows we have nothing to lose. You coming?"

His wife shakes her head. "No," she says. "Don't." But the door is already slamming behind him.

He is afraid—afraid the Healer will have already left town (*Why did I wait so long?*), more afraid that he'll find Him and inevitably discover it's all been a sham (*Why am I doing this?*). He carries the boy through the streets, trying to appear normal—as normal as a man can look awkwardly cradling his frail, unconscious, long-limbed son. He is less friendly than usual; he keeps his head down and his stride long and purposeful, hoping to give the impression that he is on an important errand. He would feel ashamed if his neighbors knew he is not even sure where he is going.

He hears the crowd before he sees it, and he veers off towards the sound of excited voices. As he gets closer, he does his best to act the part of the curious onlooker, but he is sure everyone can hear his heart pounding in his chest. He spots a man he knows from the market; they exchange greetings. "What's all the fuss about?" he shouts over the crowd.

"That Jesus fellow..." the man begins, and hope starts to swirl in the father's stomach so violently that he's afraid he might be sick. "Some of His followers are here. They call themselves his 'disciples.'"

The father stares at his acquaintance blankly for a second. "Is Jesus here?" he asks, praying that maybe he's misunderstood. But the man confirms his fears with a shake of his head. "No, no. Just a few of His friends."

The boy begins to stir in his father's arms, lifting his head a little in response to all the noise. The father turns on his heel, gripped with fury. *Idiot!* he thinks. *Of course Jesus isn't here. Why should things go our way now?* Suddenly claustrophobic, he tries to fight his way out of the throng. But he crashes into another man, someone he's never seen around town.

"Your boy is sick?" the man asks. The father shrugs his stiff shoulders. *Of course he's sick. What else could be more obvious?*

"Maybe we can heal him," says the man. He catches the eye of another man a few feet away in the crowd and gestures him over. They confer for a moment. The father clears his throat impatiently.

"Come out," one of the men says, placing his hand on the boy's damp head. "Come out."

The father stares at them, now incredulous. Who do

they think they are? The crowd is beginning to migrate towards them, and the noise increases. He looks down at his son—still listless, dark eyes open but vacant. The whole thing is feeling more and more like a cruel joke. The father begins to push his way past the men.

"Wait," one of them says. "Please wait. Let us try again." A third man emerges from the mob to join them, and again the men engage in earnest discussion. The newcomer reaches out to the boy. "I command you to come out," he says in a loud voice. He sounds confident enough, but the father notices the man's hands are trembling.

"Thanks anyway," he says, wrapping his arms protectively around his son. "We've really got to go."

He is not a man easily moved to tears, but as he struggles to break free from the crowd his vision is blurred. He is so crushingly disappointed. He feels unspeakably foolish. How will he face his wife?

He has just stepped out of the mob and taken a gulp of open air when a commotion behind him makes him turn his head. "It's Jesus!" gasps a woman in the crowd, and the people begin to press in from every direction. "Please, Healer, please, Teacher, please!" a hundred voices clamor. The father stands utterly still for a moment, every muscle tense. Has the Healer really come? Does it matter? He starts back into the crowd, then stops again. *No*, he thinks, *no. I've got to face reality.* Once more he begins fighting his way out and away from the scene.

But from the corner of his eye he can see several men gathered in a cluster, including the three would-be healers. Some of the local religious leaders are standing there too, and they are all engaged in what appears to be an intense debate—voices raised, hands gesturing wildly. And then a man—*the* man everyone seems to be trying to reach out and touch—walks up to the group and asks, "What are you arguing with them about?"

The father stops in his tracks. He knows without a doubt that the man is the Healer. "Excuse me," he says, trying to make his way over to Jesus. "Please." But the crowd is only thickening and he can't get through. He is relieved to recognize some local villagers he knows he can trust. "Keep him for me," he says, placing his son in the arms of one of the women.

His hands now free, he begins to push through the crowd more aggressively. "Out of my way!" he barks in desperation. And then somehow he finds an opening through the sea of people ("Like the parting of the Red Sea!" he will tell his wife later), and the collective motion of the crowd literally hurls him into the presence of the Healer.

I don't have to imagine what he says because the Bible records his exact words. "Teacher," he begins. Jesus looks directly into his eyes. The father is unnerved, but much to his own astonishment he continues to speak. "I brought you my son, who is possessed by a spirit that has robbed him of speech." The Healer is nodding, and the father is relieved to see that He can hear him over the noise. The words start to come out in a tumble. "Whenever it seizes him, it throws him to the ground. He foams at the mouth, gnashes his teeth, and becomes rigid." He takes a deep breath, looking for a polite way to convey the other men's failure.

"Lord," one of the men interjects. "We tried to cast the demon from this boy, but…" He stops, clears his throat. Another of the men throws his hands in the air. "Nothing happened, Lord," he cries, an edge of accusation in his voice.

"Oh unbelieving generation," Jesus says with a heavy sigh, "how long shall I stay with you? How long shall I put up with you? Bring the boy to me."

The disciples hang their heads. A few of them are mumbling under their breath. *We tried. What are we supposed to do?* The son emerges from the crowd. He has regained enough strength to walk toward his father, but the minute he sees the Healer he crashes to the ground in another convulsion.

Jesus is still looking into the eyes of the father. "How long has he been like this?" He asks, His voice deep and kind.

"From childhood," the father answers. "It has often thrown him into fire or water to kill him." Just telling the healer about the prolonged ordeal of his son's illness is an incredible release. He does not even bother to wipe away his tears. Before he knows what he is saying, he is pleading, "But if you can do anything, take pity on us and help us."

"If you can?" says Jesus. "Everything is possible for him who believes."

The father stands there in the middle of the chaos—the boy twitching on the ground, the voices crying out, the crush of hundreds of people jostling for position—and he senses that this is the defining moment of his life. Wild hope surges through him with such intensity that he fears his heart might actually burst. But there is also a despair so dark and desperate he can barely stand beneath the weight of it. Faith and doubt collide violently, and he is so unbearably torn that he is terrified he won't be able to speak. What if he fails his son? What if he fails himself?

He realizes with astonishment that he is most afraid of failing this stranger named Jesus.

He swallows hard. "I believe," he says, and though his voice is barely a whisper he knows the Healer hears him. ("I swear He looked right *through* me," he will say later, every time he tells his son the story, "and somehow I just *knew...*") He is so sure that Jesus can see straight into his conflicted heart that he adds instinctively, "Help me overcome my unbelief!"

And then Jesus looks at the boy, and though His eyes are filled with compassion His voice is stern. "You deaf and mute spirit," He says, "I command you, come out of him and never enter him again."

The boy's seizure worsens, he cries out. The convulsions go on and on. *Too long*, thinks the father, *Oh God, too long*. And then, finally, the boy is completely still, too still. "He's dead!" someone cries.

But Jesus takes the boy's hand. "Get up," He says, and now His voice is no longer stern. The boy gets up. He looks at his father, really *looks* at him, with intelligent, beautiful brown eyes. (*He has his mother's eyes*, the father realizes with a shock of joy.) And then the boy smiles. *He smiles*.

"Thank You!" cries the father. "Thank You!" But Jesus is already retreating through the crowd.[46]

———

One of the many reasons I am drawn to this story is because it contains one of the most honest prayers ever recorded. *I believe, help my unbelief!* There are moments when that is the *only* prayer I can pray.

Why do faith and doubt sometimes collide so violently within me that—like that desperate father—I am nearly torn in two? Why is it that the more my belief grows, the more I wrestle with unexpected spasms of intense unbelief?

"The truth is that the farther our faith reaches, the more doubts it encompasses, as from the highest hills there are the fullest vistas,"[47] said Malcolm Muggeridge. His words give me hope that my own pilgrimage really is progressing, even when it sometimes feels more like I am regressing or going around in circles. Could Muggeridge have actually been right when he claimed, "To believe greatly, it's necessary to doubt greatly"?[48]

I will say this, even though the admission shames me: The more I get to know God, the more He scares me. It becomes increasingly evident that He is more awesome, more wonderful, and more terrifying than I can think or imagine. He is infinitely beyond me. The more I understand, the more I see how much there is that I don't understand.

God is a mystery.

He *does* reveal much of Himself to us—through His Son, through His Word, through creation, through the Holy Spirit, and through each other. As we grow in the grace and knowledge of Him, He continues to reveal new aspects and dimensions of Himself. But however much we see, He is ever and always *more*—more than we know, more than we could handle if we did know.

All of this is good news, of course. A God we could quantify and fully comprehend would just be a really super-human, and God knows we need more than that. But we are prone to respond to the things we don't understand with fear and self-protective disbelief. Even the clues to God we find here in the natural world frighten us.

The Pythagoreans of ancient Greece were terrified when they discovered the infinite nature of irrational numbers—numbers that could only be approximated, never fully expressed in a fraction, numbers that in recent years have been computed to the six billionth decimal point without ever reaching an end. The Pythagoreans were so disturbed by their findings that they tried to keep them a secret and threatened the death penalty for anyone who revealed them. The intervening 2600 years have made the idea of infinite numbers familiar and benign to us, but I believe we still respond to fresh glimpses of anything truly eternal with Pythagorean-like terror.

The more I get to know God, the more I perceive His eternalness, His otherness. My experience of Him conforms less and less to my finite blueprint of the world. And so my knee-jerk response is fear and doubt. *This is impossible*, I think. But then I remember Jesus' words to the desperate father. "Everything is possible for him who believes."

So I work out my salvation with fear, and with trem-bling, and at the same time I remember that the God of Eternity is also the God of Love. "Perfect love drives out fear,"[49] He tells me. His words comfort me, but I know that the driving out of my fear is not likely to be an easy process.

I think of the boy convulsing and then lying on the ground like a corpse as Jesus drives the illness out of him with terrible, healing power. To be loved by God can be a terrifying thing. ("What do people mean when they say, 'I am not afraid of God because I know he is good'?" asked C.S. Lewis. "Have they never even been to a dentist?"[50]) But to be loved by God is the *only* thing. The healing it brings is worth any cost. And so I long for God even as I fear Him. And I remember the desperate father's words to Jesus. "I believe, help my unbelief."

I suspect that a great number of Christians discover as they journey with God that the more they believe—the more they perceive of God—the more doubt springs up as a natural response to the gap between what is and what is understood. To have real faith—faith that hopes for things that are not yet seen—we have to at least occasionally be confronted with a keen and painful awareness of just how unseen some of those things are. That awareness often manifests itself as doubt.

The problem is, many of us are convinced that doubt is sin, a barrier to faith. And so, in an attempt to resolve the tension, we reduce God to something we can see and understand. We tame Him, make Him safe and believable. We make Him finite. Or we elevate our own status to try to narrow the gap—make ourselves infinite, pretend we comprehend more than we do. Or we just stop thinking about it. We hang on to our earliest, most manageable ideas *about* God—filing away our salvation (like fire insurance) in a safe, secure place—but we stop getting to know God Himself. We step away from any kind of growing, dynamic relationship. Perhaps in such a state we can avoid experiencing doubt. But the victory is not only hollow, it's tragic.

When we shy away from the Mystery, when we reduce God's vast proportions to a more manageable size, we also limit our experience of wonder (which is doubt's more happily disposed twin). We deprive ourselves of the chance to stand in awe of God—completely confounded and amazed by His ways, scratching our heads, sometimes grinning, asking *How did You DO that?* We miss the chance to truly worship. We never let our fear of what we don't understand mature into the joy of knowing that there is so much more yet to come, so much more of God yet to know and love.

When I read the final verses of Romans 11, I realize that what has often been my lament (the fact that there is much about God that defies my comprehension) is Paul's Doxology.

> *Oh, the depth of the riches of the wisdom and knowledge of God! How unsearchable his judgments, and his paths beyond tracing out! "Who has known the mind of the Lord? Or who has been his counselor? Who has ever given to God, that God should repay him?" For from him and through him and to him are all things. To him be the glory forever! Amen.*[51]

Frederick Buechner said something to the effect that life is not a mystery to be *solved*, but a mystery to be *lived*. I think it can be similarly said of God that He is not a Mystery to be solved, but a Mystery to be *loved*. What He seems to want from us is a genuine relationship (He died, after all, so that we could become His friends) and an *honest* faith. Faith in the thick of doubt. Faith that *contends* with God, argues with Him, even, but never ignores Him. Faith that stumbles towards Him, rather than away from Him. Faith that remains committed to pursuing Him even when knowing Him seems to generate more questions than answers.

We will always, I suspect, experience some measure of unbelief for as long as we remain on the shadow side of eternity. Faith, like love, cannot be forced, and so to be free to believe we must also be free not to believe. We humans have been asking God to provide resounding, leave-no-room-for-doubt proof of His existence ever since we were separated from Him. We fail to understand that the provision of that kind of evidence would end His whole enterprise with us—because faith seems to be what He wants from us more than anything else, and faith in the absence of doubt would not by definition be faith.

I can't help but wonder if the disciples' belief was crippled by their refusal to admit to God, and to themselves, their own unbelief. "This kind can only come out by prayer,"[52] Jesus explained to them later, when they asked Him privately why they had failed to drive out the boy's demon. Maybe they had become so sure of their own ability to believe, so in denial about the duplicity of the human heart, that they had forgotten that they were dependent on God for even the faith to believe in Him. The father, on the other hand, was too desperate for such a charade. He came to Jesus believing just enough to trust that He would help him with his unbelief. And that, it turns out, was enough faith to move not only mountains, but the heart of God.

I Believe

Monday I felt Your hand upon my shoulder
Tuesday I felt nothing at all
Today my answers have all turned to questions
And the tears of frustration fall
Stranded in this twilight between infinite and finite
How I long to see more clearly, yet I cannot deny

That I believe that You are Someone to believe in
'Cause I believe in love
And I believe that You will help my unbelieving
And I believe that that's enough

Of all the things I thought I knew for certain
Only a very few remain
Yet some place deeper than my fear and doubting
I am still calling out Your name
So maybe there is no proof that can lead me to the whole truth
But this mystery of knowing that I cannot deny

That I believe that You are Someone to believe in
'Cause I believe in love
And I believe that You will help my unbelieving
And I believe that that's enough[53]

19

Questions
and Answers

We have a niece named Julia. She has long, raven hair and huge dark eyes. She is outrageously smart and creative. Last summer, when she was 4 and Ben was 18 months, we spent a week staying at her house in Toronto (her parents' names are on the mortgage, but it is definitely *her* house). Ben fell desperately in love with her. So did Mark and I.

Julia is in the "why" stage of life. She urgently needs and demands an explanation for anything that dares to affect her reality. Once, Mark and I happened to be upstairs during Julia's nightly bedtime ritual, and we overheard the following conversation with her daddy, Mark's brother Rick.

Rick: *Okay, Julia, it's time for bed.*

Julia: *Why?*

Rick: *Because it's eight o'clock.*

Julia: *Why?*

Rick: *Because the big hand is on the twelve and the little hand is on the eight.*

Julia: *Why?*

Rick: *Because it's eight o'clock.*

Julia: *Why?*

Rick: *Because that's how time works.*

Julia: *Why?*

Rick: *It's a long story. Anyway, you have to go to bed because you're tired.*

Julia: *Why?*

Rick: *Because little girls need sleep. Their bodies get tired, and they have to rest them so that they can keep having fun when they're awake.*

Julia: *Why?*

Rick: *Because that's the way it works.*

Julia: *Why?*

Rick: *It's a long story. You have to go to bed because I say so.*

Julia: *Why?*

Rick: *Because I love you.*

Julia: *Why?*

Rick: *Lots of reasons. Now go to sleep.*

Julia: *Why?*

Rick: *Good night.*

Julia: *Why?*

Rick: *Because. I'm turning out the light now.*

Julia (*very softly, in the dark*): *Why?*

Standing in the hallway, Mark and I tried to smother our laughter as we admired Julia's negotiating techniques. Rick tiptoed out of her room and shot us a grin. "A preview of coming attractions," he whispered, nodding his head in the direction of Ben's playpen. We knew what he meant. If Ben turns out to be half as curious and intelligent as his cousin, we'll be answering a lot of questions over the next few years. We'll have to get good at pretending we know the answers.

This, to me, is the terror of parenthood. We can teach our kids to tell time, but we can't really tell them what time *is*. We can offer everything we know about the various enterprises of our species—family, politics, art, technology, religion—but these are more the *hows* of life than the *whys*. Our children, with Julia-like determination, are bound to keep asking us questions until we are forced to resort to a rather helpless and feeble *because*. And then they'll see how little we really understand.

What will I tell my son when he realizes I have as many *whys* whistling around my soul as he does? What will I teach this boy of mine, who—just by being on the planet—has intensified both the beauty and horror of life for me?

Lately we've been going for walks at the lake. Ben picks up rocks—ordinary, dirty chunks of gravel—with a reverence that informs me they are treasures of such great value that he must take them home with him. I make a mental note to remember to empty the stuffed pockets of his jeans before I wash them. He calls to the birds and claps his hands (the way he's seen his daddy do it) to try to startle them out of their perches in the trees. His little hands make a very small sound, and the birds ignore him, but he is undaunted. There are feathers in the grass, and they are more than he could have hoped for. He throws a feather in the air and laughs with delight as the wind makes it dance.

A word like "joy" has grown archaic and almost meaningless in our culture, but when I watch Benjamin at the lake I know that joy—pure, unmitigated, irrepressible joy—exists. It wraps itself around my heart like an electric blanket.

But Benjamin is two, and two year olds are lacking an important life skill called "impulse control" (a lot of thirty-two year olds are too, but that's another story). He is overcome with an urge to run ahead, and sometimes he moves with such an astonishing burst of speed that he gets away from me and slides precariously close to the water's edge. The blood in my veins turns to ice. I snatch him to safety, of course, and we have a solemn talk about staying on the path and close to Mommy. He holds my hand, and all is well. But it takes 10 minutes for the ground to feel solid beneath my feet again—not because Ben has been in any real danger, but because I have been reminded that the danger exists. This little person's presence in the world has raised the stakes unbearably high. If something should happen to him, it is hard to imagine being able to survive it.

Life can be so wonderful, so good, that you can't help but love it passionately, can't stop yourself from throwing your arms open wide to embrace it. It is only natural to want to hold on to it forever. But the possibility always exists that it will turn on you. I remember hearing about an accident that happened in a community outside of Nashville. An air force pilot lost control of his fighter plane during a training flight and crashed through the roof of a house—a tidy house on a quiet street in a good neighborhood. The young pilot was killed—a tragedy. But I was particularly struck by the death of the middle-aged man in the house. What had he been doing that morning? Eating breakfast? Watching TV? Indulging in the guilty pleasure of sleeping in on a rare day off work? Was he the kind of guy that tried to eat right, didn't smoke, wore his seat belt, drove carefully, didn't take unnecessary chances?

There are various theories as to why most humans find life difficult, and all of them are true enough. But here, to me, is the most compelling explanation: You can do everything as right as you know how, live a good life, even trust in the God who gave it to you…and the slight possibility still exists that one day a plane could land on your house. Or your spouse could run out to the corner store for milk and never make it back home. Your child could develop a cough, and the doctor could tell you it's serious. There is no way to eliminate the risk that the existence you have learned to love with every fiber of your being might suddenly betray you.

Of course, Benjamin won't need me to tell him all the reasons life is hard. He'll come up with his own list soon enough, I'm afraid. The question is, what will he think when I tell him that for all its mess and mystery, this hard life is still a precious gift from a good God who cares when even a sparrow falls?

I desperately want my son to know that this world is not all there is, that the end will be the beginning of an existence too wonderful to imagine. I want him to be able to believe that there is a source of beauty and truth and goodness that is so absolute that it is absolutely beyond us, and yet somehow among and within us too. I want him to discover that this source is not some impersonal force of the universe but a God who knows his name. A God who thought of a boy named Benjamin Arends and spoke him into being. A God who loves him. A God who wants Benjamin Arends to love Him back.

"Son," I will tell him, "I believe these things with all of my heart and soul and mind." But what will I say when he asks me: "Why?"

What proof have I to offer? Nothing conclusive, really. I can point to the beauty of creation, the complex patterns in all of nature that seem to defy the idea of a random cosmos. I can tell him what it looks like when a baby is born—when another world collides with this one and suddenly there is a new, tiny, holy person in the room, fearfully and wonderfully made.

I can offer up my own life as evidence, and I can attempt to describe the strange but sometimes certain awareness I have that I am not alone. I can tell him that I actually communicate in some mysterious way with an unseen reality that I would bet my life is the God of the universe.

But ultimately, of course, any of this "evidence" can be explained away, and it often is. This is the dilemma of faith—it only makes sense to people who already have it. "Blessed are those who have not seen and yet have believed,"[54] Jesus said, and for any generation, operating from any given paradigm, that is a tall order. Why should we believe in something we've never seen? On what basis do we distinguish truth from delusion, and the hope of glory from desperate and rather pathetic wishful thinking?

I will tell my son a secret—something I am just now learning to believe —and it is this: The questions themselves may be the greatest proof we have that there is something *out there* beyond the cosmos (and something here in our hearts) worth believing in. Throughout the last 3000 years of documented thought, we *homo sapiens* have never come up with a way of viewing life that has kept us from asking— sometimes hopefully, sometimes despairingly, always urgently—why are we here. This is one of the strange phenomenons that distinguishes man from all other animals— we need meaning and purpose as primally as we need food and sleep. This drive is either a cruel trick of nature or the stamp of God upon our souls.

Living in the aftermath of a long list of wars, the Holocaust, and innumerable other atrocities, we bear the heavy burden of knowing the human capacity for evil. If we turn on CNN, our televisions will flicker unendingly with the evidence of ugliness in our species—tens of thousands of people starving to death daily in the Third World (while we struggle with too much food), war and poverty ravishing entire nations, and crime and disease running rampant even in our most "civilized" streets. And yet, inexplicably and indefensibly, we still search for beauty, and we even believe we find it—in paintings and in music, sometimes in churches, and in sunsets and the faces of our children. "Beauty will save the world," said Dostoyevsky, and while he may have been overstating things a bit, our quest for beauty at least suggests the possibility that the world is worth saving.

For some reason we respond to the evil around us with an instinctual, reflexive *WHY?* as if at our core we know we are meant for something better, as if even natural disasters do not seem natural—and as if there really is Someone to ask. "We experience all the horrors that go on both around us and within us *as* horrors rather than as just the way the cookie crumbles," Frederick Buechner claims, "because, in our own innermost hearts, we belong to holiness, which they are a tragic departure from."[55]

And what about time? We cannot prove that we are destined for eternity. This temporal existence—this succession of moments and hours that take us relentlessly from our beginning to a definite end—is all we've ever known. And yet the questions still rise, urgent and insistent. *What happens after we die? Where did we come from?* If this is all there is, from where did we get the ingenuity and imagination and audacity to come up with the preposterous idea of immortality?

In his *Reflections on the Psalms,* C.S. Lewis points out that our lot, the very essence of our existence, feels strangely foreign to us.

> *We are so little reconciled to time that we are even astonished at it. "How he's grown!" we exclaim, "How time flies!" as though the universal form of our experience were again and again a novelty. It is as strange as if a fish were repeatedly surprised at the wetness of water. And that would be strange indeed; unless of course the fish were destined to become, one day, a land animal.*[56]

And what of our questions about the existence of God? Our preoccupation with who may or may not be out there might be attributed merely to social conditioning, but if there is nothing but an impersonal void beyond this world, why did it ever occur to any man to think otherwise?

Would there be any atheists if there were no God to not believe in?

To be alive and human is to ask these questions: *Why is there evil in the world? Is there life beyond this one? Are we alone in the cosmos? What is man that God should be mindful of us? What is God that we should be mindful of Him?* We ask them of life, and life asks them of us. They rise, unbidden, from the depths of our souls, and I believe they tell us that we are meant for something—or Someone—holy and eternal.

"In every man is a God-shaped vacuum," Pascal said, and if I understand him correctly, he was telling us that the aching chasm inside ourselves is the best evidence we have that we are in need of something beyond ourselves. Calling this vacuum "God-shaped" may seem like a leap, unless of course you encounter a God whom you cannot prove exists, but nonetheless fits the hole in your soul like a key in a lock. This, I will tell my son, is how it has been for me. And if he struggles to believe my answer, I will ask him to listen to the questions rumbling deep within his own soul, and I will pray they tell him more than answers ever could.

He alone is capable of making Himself known as He really is; we search in reasoning and in the sciences, as in a poor copy, for what we neglect to see in an excellent original. God Himself paints Himself in the depths of our souls.

Brother Lawrence

Postlude

*Listen, I tell you a mystery. We will not all
sleep, but we will all be changed—in a flash, in the
twinkling of an eye, at the last trumpet. For the trumpet will
sound, the dead will be raised
imperishable, and we will be changed.*

1 Corinthians 15:51-52

*All shall be well and all shall be well and
all manner of thing shall be well.*

Lady Julian of Norwich

20

The Delivery Room

(worth the trip)

I hate disappointment. Everyone does, of course, but I've been known to go to rather extravagant lengths to avoid it. My motto: It is better to be pleasantly surprised than bitterly disappointed. My strategy: Don't count your chickens until they've hatched, grown, and shown every indication they're going to lead a long and healthy life.

When I thought I might be pregnant, I didn't mention it to a soul. The day I went to the supermarket to pick up a pregnancy test, I convinced myself I was going for gum. I also bought a magazine, some contact solution, four packs of light bulbs, and several other items I didn't want or need—all decoys. I guess I was attempting to divert the checkout clerk's attention from the true matter at hand—after all, there was no point disappointing her if the test came out negative.

I brought the test home and followed the instructions meticulously—all the while telling myself I already knew the (negative) outcome. I waited two excruciating minutes before the bathroom began to spin. I checked the pamphlet: one line means negative, two lines mean positive. I checked the test: two lines. I checked the test again: still two lines. TWO LINES.

By the time Mark came home I'd been crying helplessly for at least an hour. He dropped his car keys and asked me to please, please tell him what was wrong. I was too overcome to explain that nothing was wrong at all—something was incredibly, terrifyingly, miraculously right. "I have news," I whispered. "Guess."

"You got the Visa bill," he tried, his voice taut with concern. I shook my head. "Phone bill?" he ventured, beginning to get truly frightened. "No," I managed, "nothing like that." He was approaching panic. His face turned gray. "The car. What happened to the car?"

Now I was angry enough to pull myself together a little and put my lips to his ear. "Listen, you big jerk. I'm going to have your baby."

We spent the next several minutes watching the room spin together, hanging onto each other for dear life. We kissed. We prayed. We tried to determine what parents-to-be do, exactly, and decided we should probably go discuss it at our favorite Italian restaurant. I ordered a glass of milk for the first time in 15 years.

In accordance with my anti-disappointment philosophy, we resolved to keep our news a secret from all but our closest family members until we were safely past the first trimester. No one suspected a thing. After all, we'd been married and deftly avoiding parenthood for eight years. Around the five-year mark, concerned friends and family had asked subtly if we might need a how-to book, but since then everyone had pretty much given up on us.

We knew my parents would be ecstatic to learn that at last we were making them first-time grandparents, so we gave ourselves permission to drop them a couple of enormous hints. We presented them each with a gift. We gave my mom a photo album—it just happened to have "Grandma's Brag Book" inscribed on the cover. We gave my dad a couple of chocolate cigars—one with a pink ribbon, one with a blue ribbon. They opened their packages and stopped breathing. I think they were afraid we might be playing some sort of cruel joke. "Really?" gasped my mom. We assured them we weren't kidding, and then we all hugged and watched the room spin some more.

The great lie they tell expectant mothers is that it takes nine months to grow a baby. It actually takes forty weeks—ten long months lived in a parallel universe where each day is as a thousand years. My resolve not to get too excited or filled with anticipation was broken almost as quickly as my "never throw up in public" rule.

The little person inside my body was making his presence felt more emphatically every day. The doctors showed us pictures—ultrasonic images so blurry they had to label the body parts for us. We had never seen anything more beautiful in our lives. And they placed a device on my watermelon of a belly and broadcast my baby's heartbeat—a strong, steady pulse that seemed to come from some distant galaxy, or from dreams I didn't even know I'd been dreaming, or from heaven itself.

I couldn't wait to meet him, and I thought there was a very good chance the suspense would kill me. But as my due date approached, I began to wonder how my baby would feel about his journey into the world. After all, he would have my genetic code to contend with, and the only thing I hate more than disappointment is change.

Maybe it's laziness, or lack of courage. Maybe it's due to the fact that my family moved six times before I entered the eighth grade. For whatever reason, I strongly prefer to have things remain the same. I would not, for example, let Mark shave his mustache for at least a year past the point he felt it was no longer fashionable. He'd had facial hair for as long as I'd known him, and I didn't see any reason to make rash alterations. (He eventually overruled me, and I'm happy to report that he has a lovely upper lip.) I've been wearing the same beloved pair of comfortable black boots for three years now, despite my worried friend Bernie's warning that they are listing dangerously to the starboard side.

If my baby took after me even a little, he was going to be understandably resistant to any changes in his environment.

After all, he'd been living in the same cozy spot for nine (make that ten) months now—a safe, familiar place featuring excellent temperature control and prearranged meals. The outside world couldn't seem too inviting—strange, bright, noisy, and filled with intrusive grandparent paparazzi. His journey away from the only home he'd ever known would be terrifying.

Whether my baby thought it was a good idea or not, thankfully there was no stopping nature. At last my body began its mysterious labor—from the first contraction, I knew it was serious. We made it to the hospital in a nervous blur and set up camp in a delivery room. It was harder, messier, and more awe-inspiring than we ever dreamed. And our anticipation mounted to unbearable levels as every surreal hour brought us closer to meeting our little boy.

At some point the bright lights, the voices of the nurses, my husband's sweet face, and even the pain all became a backdrop to the conversation I was having with my baby. "Don't worry," I told him, trying to send messages down the umbilical cord. "I know this is scary, but I promise it will be worth it. This is the world you're meant to live in. And there are so many people here who cannot wait to see you, and love you, and show you around."

I have no idea if he heard or understood me. But he came. And he did not disappoint. He had something of me in his eyes, and a lot of his daddy everywhere else, but he was thoroughly, perfectly, exquisitely himself. And we were so glad to meet him.

It was a few weeks before I thought again about the dialogue I'd had with Benjamin while he was making his way to my arms. I was rocking him to what I desperately hoped would be sleep, exhausted but still astounded by his presence. I was thinking about how many hearts he'd captured already in his short life, and I wondered with a twinge of sadness what my granddad, and Rich, and the few other loved ones I've already lost would have thought of him. Could they see how beautiful he was from heaven?

Ben was squirming in my embrace, his eyes open and impossibly blue, his skin like moonlight. It struck me that the trip that begins this life might resemble the one that ends it more than we imagine. It's only natural to fear the unknown, and when it's time for me to go, I suspect I will resist—terrified as always of change and disappointment. But if the One who made my beautiful boy really has prepared a place for us, surely the journey will be worth it.

Benjamin is changing far too quickly, growing too fast. But there is still something like angel dust glistening in his downy hair, and there are times I find myself wondering if he isn't somehow a message sent to me from the world that dreamed him up. Some nights, watching him sleep, I feel certain we are both cradled in a stronger embrace, and I cannot help but believe that he and I—all of us—are meant for more than this world.

Yet death, like life, remains a mystery—as much of a mystery as the terrible, consuming, wonderful love of God. I am afraid of it. Once again, the best is what I understand least. But I am learning to believe that death, like all the Divine Mysteries, is not a wall that shuts me out, but a door that ushers me in. The end of this life is not the final chapter. But it *is* the final question. It is the chance to live into the Answer.

A few nights ago Benjamin's daddy, my Mark, rolled over in bed and touched my hand. He was not yet asleep, but not really awake, either—suspended in that dreamlike state one travels through for a few precious seconds before diving into slumber. "Do you think, when we get there, we'll ask God all our questions?" he whispered in the dark. "Or will we just say...*holy, holy, holy*. just...*holy, holy, holy?*"

And then we fell asleep.

Now we see but a poor reflection as in a mirror; then we shall see face to face. Now I know in part; then I shall know fully, even as I am fully known.

1 Corinthians 13:12

Acknowledgments

If you have read this book, you know that I owe a rather enormous debt to my family. I would like to specifically thank them here for letting me write about them, and for hardly ever asking me to censor anything.

Mark stayed up with me way too late on way too many nights; it was clear that I could not write this book without him.

Joy Jonat (my mother) provided essential editorial input upon the completion of every chapter, and she never charged me a penny.

It is strange that there is not a chapter about my friend Nicole Udzenija—her startling insights have influenced the way I see the world for many years.

I must thank Bernie Sheahan for her genius and her friendship. To call her my "twin" is to flatter myself, but I do it anyway. She is the one who convinced me there was a "proser" lurking deep within me...so if you don't like this book, send your letters to her.

Many people were generous and patient beyond what could be reasonably expected in helping me to grapple with the mess and the mystery of both my life and my manuscript. I am thinking specifically of the Spenci—Spencer Capier and Spencer Welch—my bandmates and teachers. The epiphanies of many a conversation hollered above the roar of plane engines are reflected in these pages. I must also thank Roy Salmond, who told me at a critical juncture that it was OK to doubt and encouraged the asking of questions. Email dialogues with Rose Capanna were invaluable. The members of the Carolyn Arends Email Newslist—maintained by Joan Slonecker—helped me in the early stages of this book by sharing the things they wonder most about God. And The Enthusiasts have given me much to think and laugh about.

Many friends will recognize their own thoughts and words in these pages—Connie Harrington, Brad Crisler, Lisa Eller, Sally Jones, Kathy Bubel, and Troy VanLiere come to mind, and there are several others who shall remain nameless but appreciated.

Blue Mountain Baptist Church no longer has orange-cushioned pews, but it remains an excellent place to explore the Mystery. I thank my pew-mates, as well as Pastor Curt and Pastor Cam (and Pastors past such as Lee and John).

Vicki Jennette stood in the gap for me on many a dark and stormy night, and when I could not believe I would ever finish this book, she believed for me.

Lisa Bergren took me seriously as a writer long before it was reasonable to do so—therefore she too shares some of the blame for this endeavor.

Conversations with Ron Arends helped to spark this book. Although he and I have come to different conclusions, his keen intelligence has assisted me in learning which questions need asking.

Seven years ago, Pete Fisher, Dan Raines, Jeanie Kaserman, and Roberta Croteau helped me navigate my authorship safely to Harvest House's shores. I am most grateful to Carolyn McCready and Terry Glaspey for not running away screaming when I said I wanted to write a book about mess and mystery. Terry was (and is) a patient, insightful, and incredibly well-read editor. Kim Moore and Barb Gordon were likewise helpful.

I am grateful to the visionaries at ConversantLife.com (including Stan Jantz, Bruce Bickel, and Peter Schumerth) for starting this new conversation. Speaking of new conversations, I've shared many with Paula Flink over the past few years, and she's developed both my filing system and my laugh muscles in wonderful ways.

Finally, to you, dear readers, thank you for spending this time with me. *"May the Lord of peace himself give you peace at all times and in every way. The Lord be with all of you"* (2 Thessalonians 3:16).

Go with God,
Carolyn Arends

Notes

Wrestling

1. Stan Meissner, theme song for "The Berenstain Bears" TV show, copyright © 2002, Nelvana (Toronto, CAN). Used by permission.
2. Frederick Buechner, *The Magnificent Defeat* (San Francisco: HarperSanFrancisco, 1985), 12.
3. Genesis 32:22-29.

Wrestling with Angels

1. "Reaching," words and music by Carolyn Arends, © Copyright 1995 New Spring Publishing, Inc. (ASCAP) (a div. of Brentwood-Benson Music Publishing, Inc.)/running arends music (ASCAP) (admin. by Peermusic Ltd.). All rights reserved. Used by permission.
2. G.K. Chesterton, *Orthodoxy* (New York, NY: Doubleday, 1990), p. 9.
3. From "Graceland," words and music by Paul Simon, © 1986 Paul Simon. Used by permission of the publisher: Paul Simon Music.
4. Job 38:4 7.
5. Job 38:8-11.
6. Job 38:31-33.
7. Job 38:34-38.
8. "It Has to Be You," words and music by Carolyn Arends, © copyright 1994, New Spring Publishing, Inc. (ASCAP) (a div. of Brentwood-Benson Music Publishing, Inc.) All rights reserved. Used by permission.
9. 1 Samuel 7:6.
10. 1 Samuel 7:8.
11. 1 Samuel 7:10.
12. 1 Samuel 7:12.
13. Luke 23:42.
14. 1 Samuel 1:8.
15. 1 Samuel 1:11.
16. 1 Samuel 1:17.
17. 1 Samuel 1:19.
18. www.alzheimers.com, The Basics, "What Is Alzheimer's Disease?"
19. From "Blessed Assurance," words by Fanny J. Crosby, music by Phoebe P. Knapp.

20. From "When We All Get to Heaven," words by Eliza E. Hewitt, music by Emily D. Wilson.

21. From "In the Sweet By and By," words by S.F. Bennett, music by J. P. Webster.

22. Romans 8:38-39.

23. Revelation 4:8.

24. C.S. Lewis, *Letters to Malcolm: Chiefly on Prayer* (New York, NY: Harcourt Brace Jovanovich, 1964), p. 75.

25. Romans 5:8.

26. Matthew 10:39.

27. Matthew 19:30.

28. Mark 10:43-44.

29. Matthew 5:5.

30. Romans 12:2.

31. G.K. Chesterton, *Orthodoxy* (New York, NY: Doubleday, 1990), p. 29.

32. Matthew Henry, *Matthew Henry's Commentary on the Bible* (Peabody, MA: Hendrickson Publishers, 1997).

33. From "Elijah," words and music by Rich Mullins, © Meadowgreen Music, Inc., (ASCAP), 1983.

34. John Irving, *A Prayer for Owen Meany* (New York, NY: William Morrow and Company, Inc., 1989), p. 543.

35. Matthew 10:39.

36. Ron Reed, Loren Wilkinson, Tim Anderson, et al., *Dreams of Kings and Carpenters*.

37. Ibid.

38. Ibid.

39. Isaiah 9:6 (KJV).

40. Matthew 2:18.

41. Loren Wilkinson, "Rachel" from *Dreams of Kings and Carpenters*.

42. Ron Klug, "Joseph's Lullaby" from *The Country of the Risen King* (ed. Merle Meeter), Baker Book House.

43. Luke 2:10-11.

44. John 15:13.

45. Proverbs 13:12.

46. This story can be found in Mark 9:14-27.

47. Malcolm Muggeridge, *The End of Christendom* (Grand Rapids, MI: Wm. B. Eerdmans Publishing Company, 1990), p. 5.

48. Ibid., p. 27.

49. I John 4:18.

50. C.S. Lewis, *A Grief Observed* (New York, NY: Bantam, 1961), pp. 50-51.

51. Romans 11:33-36.

52. Mark 9:29.

53. "I Believe," words and music by Carolyn Arends, © Copyright 1994 New Spring Publishing, Inc. (ASCAP) (a div. of Brentwood-Benson Music Publishing, Inc.) All rights reserved. Used by permission.

54. John 20:29.

55. Frederick Buechner, *The Eyes of the Heart* (New York, NY: HarperSanFrancisco, 1999), p. 16.

56. C.S. Lewis, *Reflections on the Psalms* (New York, NY: Harcourt, Brace & World, 1958), p. 138.

About the Author

Carolyn Arends has released nine albums and is the author of two critically acclaimed books. Fifteen of Arends' songs have become top 10 radio singles on the Canadian pop and U.S. Christian charts. Arends has earned two Dove Awards, three Juno Nominations, and was recognized as the West Coast Music Awards' Songwriter of the Year.

Accolades aside, Arends is known for songs and books that stir the soul, and a warm, engaging style that leave her audiences feeling like they've found a new best friend. "I don't write songs and books as much as I get ambushed by them," Arends confesses. "And I write primarily about God because he is what captivates my imagination. The idea that we can know the Creator of the Universe, and that he knows us...I simply can't think of any more fascinating subject matter."

Discography

- Pollyanna's Attic
- Christmas: An Irrational Season
- Under the Gaze
- We've Been Waiting for You (The Parenthood Project)
- Travelers
- Seize the Day and Other Stories
- This Much I Understand
- Feel Free
- I Can Hear You

Arends graduated from Trinity Western University in Langley, B.C. with a degree in psychology and English. She lives in British Columbia with her husband, Mark, and their children Ben and Bethany.

Bring Carolyn Arends
to Your Community!

Speaking and Retreat Ministry
Songwriting and Performance Seminars and Workshops
Concerts
Worship Leading

Contact Running Arends Music
1-866-953-1833, booking@carolynarends.com, or
www.carolynarends.com

•

Speaking and Retreat Ministry

I want to thank you for your ministry at our Family Camp...The theme you followed was uplifting and personally challenging; it was a perfect fit for what we wanted. Your teaching exhibited a heart for God and was enhanced by your PowerPoint presentation and a beautiful blending in of your music . . . Many expressed a deep appreciation for the content and style of your presentations. They were blessed as I was.

Don Swanson, Camp Nakamun

Songwriting and Performance Seminars and Workshops

Carolyn brings the gift of craftsmanship, sensitivity to the heart of an artist, wisdom forged in the fires of experience, and a godly passion to bring out the best in every songwriter. I recommend Carolyn's teaching without exception.

Arlen Salte, BreakForth Ministries

Concerts

I was mesmerized with Carolyn's concert. It was intimate and personal and seemed like spending an evening with a good friend.

Fan, Ottawa

Worship Leading

Carolyn has a gift in reaching the inner heart of a woman to be opened to our Lord and how He ministers to that heart. She has a special way of connecting the spirits of women to the King.

Pat Portman, Women's Ministries Pastor,
Central Peninsula Church, California

It's a Harsh,

Crazy,

Beautiful,

Messed Up,

Breathtaking

World...

And People Are Talking About It...

conversant **life** .com

engage your faith